W9-CQC-015

THE MIRACLE OF BEING THE REAL YOU

Irene Amanda Hunter

The Real You Publishing
Phoenix, Arizona

Copyright, ©2001 by Irene Amanda Hunter

Second printing, 2005

All rights exclusively reserved. No part of this book may be reproduced or translated into any language or utilized in any form or by any means, electronic or mechanical, including photocopying, recording or by any information storage and retrieval system, without permission in writing from the publisher.

The Real You Publishing, LLC
Phoenix, Arizona

ISBN 0-9673714-0-6

Book design by Michael Campbell, Campbell Fisher Design, Phoenix, AZ; Typesetting by Michele DeFilippo, 1106 Design, LLC, Phoenix, AZ

The information presented in this book is intended to inform, educate, enlighten and inspire. The author and publisher shall have neither liability nor responsibility to any person or entity with respect to any loss or damage caused, or alleged to be caused, directly or indirectly by the information contained in this book.

Printed in the United States of America

– Contents –

Figures

Foreword

Irene Amanda Hunter is legendary! The "legend" of Irene evolved through many eras, time zones, and cultures. In my culture, she is the woman who took the same thirty-week spirituality course *seven* times — to make sure she got it right. This book is evidence that she did indeed get it right. Irene has been teacher, counselor, mentor, and friend to thousands. Working through various businesses, spiritual education centers, churches, and in her own home over the past thirty years, she has gifted so many with the wisdom that *you* now hold in your hands. We who have looked at the same ragged flip chart pages of drawings and diagrams in her living room for the past twenty years are most grateful to have them in a hand-held size!

As I read this work, I kept revisiting my own fifteen years of classes and private sessions with Irene and experiencing afresh the clarity she brings to assist us in creating a good and fulfilled life. Her writing reflects my experience of her. Her sentences feel like the rapid-fire instruction I received in her classes. Her guidance through the maze of the human thought and feeling processes is clear, multi-dimensional, and effective in bringing resolution to the most puzzling questions. Her illustrations open the door on profound insights into our many-layered selves.

Some of her personal clients call her "Sergeant Love." She listens attentively and lovingly — and then WHAM! she tells you the Truth of the situation. With certainty and strength, Irene points you toward resolution. (That's the "Sergeant" part.) In truth, Irene is so convinced that the wisdom she gives in this book is real, clear, and so "right on," that she will face any dragon or foe to take a stand for the spiritual Truth that sets us all free. (That's the "Love" part.) One of her statements that I have applied to many aspects of my life is, "If you really love them, you will stand their wrath and disappointment, and stay in principle anyway."

Irene has stood in the wrath and disappointment of students *and* colleagues who did not want to hear or apply the principles (laws) that she details here. She has done so because she is a woman of great love, passion, and compassion. Even as we argued with her, tried to prove her wrong, and assured her that we understood all she was saying and that it just didn't apply to us, she lovingly kept repeating these eternal truths until we either opened up enough to really try them and accept them, or we just surrendered. You will see some of the ideas herein repeated throughout. Know that this is not an error. Get it! Accept it! Apply it!

While Irene is a legend, she is not a guru. She would rather send a student or client away than to have them dote on her words and not challenge them. She can relate these lessons to us because she has applied herself to them throughout her life — and continues to do so. This is not static information, but a vibrant, living wisdom. It is up to us to embody it, apply it, test it, and reflect it in the world as our own happy, successful, and inspiring lives. My life is richer because of this teaching, and I have dared to pass along to my own students the simplicity and profundity of this work.

This book is a blessing. These teachings are real-time guidelines for life. It is time that these clear and direct statements get into the hands of more people. Initially, the most grateful people will be Irene's own students who have waited a long time to get all those flip chart pages into regular size print! The next layer of those blessed by it will be our students to whom we can now give a direct dose of Irene's guidance. Finally, there is the rest of the world. Everyone everywhere can apply these universal laws of Truth and create exciting and fulfilling lives. This book does not offer hope. It provides pathways that, when followed, lead to the vibrant and active awakening of The Real You.

— Rev. Kathryn E. McDowell

Foreword

A sage once said, "When the student is ready, the teacher appears." It seems like centuries ago when my life seemed so unbalanced I was about to tip over and spill garbage I had been gathering and storing, and a friend of mine advised me to take Irene Hunter's The Real You seminar. My friend said, "I have been a psychiatric nurse for more than twenty years, and I've seen many, many programs. Her course is the only one that works."

Taking The Real You course is the best thing I could have done for myself and for everyone in my life. It worked then, and twenty-plus years later, it is still working. Irene's dedication and commitment to her life's work as a spiritual teacher have helped hundreds of others find themselves. Her teachings are a direct, practical guide to self-empowerment. Her love for all in life, no matter what face it wears, is demonstrated by her ongoing support, guidance, and instruction. She lives what she teaches, and she teaches what she lives.

Although her work often is cloaked in the nature of one, Irene is no angel; her stature transcends that. She's a teacher of the highest quality. Time and time again, I have seen her work with students who came to her feeling that their lives were nearly in a pile of rubble. Step by step, as she indicates in this book, the trash is sorted, identified, and is cast off, and The Real You is revealed. From broken parts and poverty of self-acceptance arises personal prosperity and wholeness.

The reason The Real You course works is because it goes to the core of Who you are inside and teaches you how to recall that goodness and pureness with which you entered this life. It focuses on solutions while it teaches the student to recognize and face problems, then instructs you how to let go of them to discover the Truth of you.

Irene Hunter's courses have done that for me and for thousands of others. In her course, The Real You, Irene gives you the greatest gift of all — your Self.

— Nancy M. Brannon
Cave Creek, Arizona

Introduction

This book offers a road map to your inner potential, your real power, your soul's journey.

An understanding, a knowledge of the Spiritual Self (The Real You) changes your life continuously by inspiring, supporting, healing, guiding, guarding, and protecting you like no person, place, or thing can ever do for you. The deep trust and security you search for is in this inner, mysterious Source of Power. That you can depend on!

This book is experiential, so the approach is one of test and measuring the premises, tools, and concepts. See how they can make a difference in your life immediately. For example apply the principle that "now is all there is." When you adjust your thinking to take care of "just now," stress is released, you are more vital and centered, more effective and efficient doing the task at hand. The life energy flows.

"You" is deliberately used all through the book rather than "we." When you read it with the concept that it is The Real You, your Inner Self, talking to you and teaching you, you will be more comfortable with the approach. The Real You reveals Itself to you, and the false self disappears, and your belief systems change for the better. In reality, there is only "you," and what is around you is the mirror reflection of your consciousness.

I have tested these principles in my own life and in The Real You Seminars for more than forty-five years, and I have experienced and witnessed miraculous changes in my students' lives.

This is a book of empowerment, of taking charge of your life and succeeding. Your inner self shows you why you must love yourself with all your heart and all your might before you can love anyone else. Self-esteem and self-acceptance, The Real You, are the keys to reverence for life and its unique expression in all forms. They work.

Throughout the text, there is repetition of the important points and laws. I think these concepts are so vital to the great life that they need repeating in different contexts.

— Love and Light,

Irene

Acknowledgments

It is with the utmost gratitude I acknowledge Nancy Brannon for her years of tenacious efforts to get this book from my head and into your hands. Without her, it was just a dream that I had. She graciously offered her time and talents to get it down on paper, and she stuck with me through the hours and hours of rewriting. What an angel.

I extend my gratitude also to longtime students, Reverend Kathryn McDowell, Jemma Kopel, and Margaret Critchley-Patterson for their efforts in editing and suggestions. I am thankful for the encouragement of many students who believed in the book. Thank you, Michael Campbell, one of the greatest graphic artists alive today for his gift of the cover. I honor Dr. Mark Carpenter, a minister from Religious Science Church, my beloved teacher for so many years.

I give thanks to my husband, James E. Hunter, whose love and passion for "The Real You" kept me motivated.

This book is dedicated to my sons,

Fire Chief Karl M. Keierleber

and

Gilbert Kim Keierleber,

and to my grandchildren,

Joseph Keierleber

Jesse Keierleber

Natalie Keierleber

SandraKeierleber

Stephen Keierleber

Karlene Hunter

Ryan Helton

Brandon Helton

Erin Sicher

Marc Hunter and

Eddie Hunter.

1

Discovering the Real You

Chapter One

Basic Concepts of Individuality

There is a Power and Presence within you right now that is greater than you are. It is the Real You, and you can direct It, for you are a Spiritual Being in the human experience, not a human being searching for Spirit. You are a complete, whole, totally self-contained unit of the Universal Life Force, right now. You are an individualized expression of the creative process. You came into this world through birth and will leave through death. Birth and death are but the framework of your journey here. The Real You is not only invisible, it is also immeasurable.

Who Am I?

To study yourself is the most important investigation you will ever make. For right where you are now, you have everything you need to become that successful person you were born to be. By seeing through your life games and thought patterns, you begin to glimpse the power and potential that reside within your True Being. Your personal expression of this Life Energy can be positive or negative. You set up your own law of attraction by your choice of words and thoughts. These words and thoughts can attract or repel your good in all of your life experiences. It is very beneficial that you know your personality traits as they really are, not as you may think them to be. By closely examining the aspects of attitudes, adjustability, emotional control, impulse control, purpose, sensitivity, and self-integrity, you can make changes that will bring your false self into alignment with the Real You. This is creative living, here and now.

You are your own authority. This is true for you whether or not you know it, believe it, or accept it. The final authority is yours. You decide what role is yours and what role you will let others play in your life. You decide what information you accept, what habits you develop, what thoughts you think, and what kind of life you live. Since you do, in actuality, exercise final authority in your life, you can gain greater control over your life when you recognize that you are exercising this control and authority.

When you really realize that the responsibility for your life begins and ends with you, then you start treating all forms of information, including conversations, reading material, television, and radio with more care, and you become an actor rather than a reactor. That is, you act with deliberation and you then start getting the results that bring you what you need to be a successful, happy, secure person.

Your world and your reality, or consciousness, is bound by your knowledge and experience. This is a wonderful universe, full of Power to do things, and that Power is within you. This Power can bring you great freedom and happiness.

Take control of your own life. Take control of your own mind. Recognize your supreme authority over yourself. You'll find that in doing so, you no longer desire to exercise control over someone else's life.

Don't count on other people, count on yourself. Now is the time to stop counting on other people to help make your life happy and secure. Now is the time to stop counting on certain places or the possessing of certain things to make your life happy and secure. Don't force other people to fit your mold and to be moral or intelligent by your definition. You are the only one who can fit your mold. Take the responsibility for your life and utilize the source of the Real Power that exists for you, within you.

You will find that there are many ways to get what you want without manipulating other people or going through other people. When you rely upon person, place, or thing to achieve a certain result for you, the freedom and happiness to be achieved by you is limited to those persons, places, or things; and you have really limited your freedom and happiness by their limits.

Your real power lies in your power to decide for yourself and to exercise your final authority over your world. You are the ruler of your world, and the sooner you realize it and start acting and believing in yourself as the ruler of your world, the sooner you will start making the decisions that bring you happiness and freedom.

Let the Real You have the freedom to express. The Real You does not seek to compete, compare, or judge. The Real You does not seek approval. Your greatest moment is experienced when you can be your Real Self, and thus feel free to enjoy the good things that life has to offer you. Letting the Real You express is a skill. To know yourself and to cast off the habits and cover-ups that have been building up for a lifetime can happen overnight or can take some period of readjustment. The Real You is a relaxed person who knows how to act in ways consistent with the real nature of you.

The Real You is unique. Let your uniqueness shine through and it will be appreciated by others. Let this come forth naturally without force or manipulation. Just be you in a natural way, without drawing attention to the fact that you are in any way attempting to demonstrate to others that you are different. The difference and uniqueness shows automatically.

Your life is what you make of it. *Thoughts are things,* and thought by thought, you are exercising your ability to think in accordance with or against your true nature. *You become what you think.* The choice is really yours. You can choose love, peace, poise, power, prosperity, health; or you can choose tensions and pressure, strain and struggle, hurts and heartaches. You can change your attitudes! Life is nothing more than change. Some lives are like a cemetery, they take in everything and give out nothing. You are here to experience the full awareness of life. The great essential for this freedom is the correct point of view, the correct attitude, the correct understanding.

The purpose of this book is to help you see the relationship between the way you think and how it affects what is happening to you. *Change your thinking, and change your life!* The techniques presented to you here will help you train your brain, which is not your mind, but is an instrument of your mind, and to tap into, direct, and focus on the Super Intelligence within you. You will discover that your purpose for existing is to be more of who you really are — your importance as a center of Life Energy that is ever-expressing. You are a being becoming. You are a totally self-contained unit. You have all the Power and patterns within you to become the Real You now. The Real You is a self-actualized person building a strong support system within to accomplish and sustain self-realization and to be self-reliant.

The universal cosmic system in which you are immersed is Divine Life Energy or Divine Intelligence in action. That same Intelligence that flows in and through the plants, in and through the birds and bees also flows in and through you right now. You are an integral part of the universal system. Everyone and everything is connected in the universal system of Power and Pattern in a unity consciousness. Life Energy flows through everything and everyone in the universe. It's common to all forms. It is in this "that" we are all one.

As the highest form of energy that exists on planet earth, you can think. Other forms may think, but they are not aware of their thoughts. The human being is aware of thoughts, and that sets them apart from other life forms that exist. So your world is shaped by your thinking. What are your thoughts creating for you? *What thinking has done, thinking can undo.*

The basic principle is, *thoughts are things.* Every thought you think is moving its energy into form, whether you're aware of it or not. Everything that you see was a pattern in the invisible before it became visible. Even you were. Everything that expresses in form has its own uniqueness. Every thumbprint is different. You are an important part of the whole design.

Your experience is related to thought, which is constantly directing this Divine Intelligence, moment by moment, into forms that you manifest in your life. As you observe this universal process, it becomes obvious that there is a Perfect Timing, Perfect Harmony, Perfect Balance, Perfect Order. Power and Pattern exist in all things.

When you are in tune with the universal process, you are centered within your world. You are healthy, happy, joyful. Everything is right, and you are flowing. But when your thinking process has been misused or you have accepted thoughts that really don't belong, you begin to experience frustration, anxiety, poverty, poor health. All of these things are created by the thoughts that you bring into the system and accept as being your truth. The invisible becomes visible, the formless becomes form, cause (inner) becomes effect (outer), thought becomes thing; and what thinking has done, thinking can undo.

Choice

Human beings can choose. Everything else must be what it is. For example, within an acorn, even though you can't see it, is the Power, the creative energy, and a pattern, but no choice. Everything in the universe is power and pattern. Within the acorn is the pattern of the oak tree. Plant the acorn in the soil, give it tender loving care, and it will produce an oak tree. That's its purpose, that's its function, even though it is invisible. It's not going to change its mind and grow lemons on one branch and figs on another. It can't shed its leaves because it's angry with the farmer. It doesn't have moods. It simply is what it is and it does what it can with what it can take from the environment. It produces at the highest and finest and best it can without comparison, competition, seeking approval, or judgement. It simply does its thing.

You, too, have within you a unique pattern. You have all the Power that you can accept and use. It exists around you, moving in and through you. At the level of your thought is the level at which you are experiencing this power in your life.

Everything that is happening to you is a result of you being you. If things are not going well for you, and you're blaming your parents, society, or life, you're in the wrong ball park. Everything that is happening to you is a result of your choices. Any negativity is a result of you not taking charge of your thinking, of not expressing thoughts that assist you in achieving what you desire to experience.

You are the captain of your ship. For the remainder of this book, think of yourself as an individualized space on planet earth. You are moving about, enveloped in an energy that you can direct with your own authority. This is true for every person. You'll never be an authority over someone else and be free. Any time you control another person, that person in turn controls you, like a ball and chain.

It is important to dehypnotize yourself from outer controls of places, of people, of things. Now you can take charge of the conditions and the experiences that are taking place in your life. You can stop reacting to life (which creates victims), and take action on your terms (get your power back). You do have choice. Because humans are the highest form of energy, they are meant to have dominion over their world, as long as they flow with the natural principles of the universe.

It doesn't matter who you're thinking about or who you're projecting your thoughts upon, they are your thoughts. You're thinking them, energizing those thought patterns, and bringing them into your experience. It is called the law of attraction. *The law of attraction brings to you what you are thinking.*

Being in control of your own space, taking care of that space, and doing your own thing are not irresponsible, self-centered, and selfish actions. When you are being real and being truthful and honest with yourself and doing your highest and finest, the paradox is that you flow in harmony with everything else that is doing its highest and finest and best.

Your life purpose is to express your highest potential, that Perfect Pattern that is the Real You. That pattern is not set like it is in the acorn. That pattern in you is determined by choice. You can choose different dramas, different concepts, or different ways of life to express. It always operates as Law, Love, Pattern, and Power at the level of your acceptance. And when you are expressing your divine essence, you are automatically a success. You flow in harmony with every other human being on this level because of the magnetic law of attraction. *You attract to you what you are.*

Everything in your experience is a result of your thought processes to this moment in time. If you don't like something, change the thoughts behind it. Take time to become aware of those patterns that you're holding in place. Your thought patterns set up a magnetic force and bring experiences and situations into your life.

Through practical application, you can now test the concepts in areas of your life that need to be brought to a higher and better experience. Examine the areas in which you're succeeding to see where you are thinking correctly to create a right experience for you. That includes everything — when you're at a traffic light and it's red or green, when you're late for a meeting, when you're entering an unknown experience, or maybe your life has taken a tremendous change — all of these things are generated by your thoughts, your choices!

Change

The whole universe, all of nature, is in constant motion, ever changing and ever becoming more of what it is. Change is inevitable and is built into the world process. Your resistance to it will cause your own destruction. No relationship, no situation, no event is permanent. Change is as certain as the rising and setting of the sun and moon. It is as certain as breathing. If you remain static, it is because you are static and stagnant in your thinking. You can learn to flow by daring to participate in this life process. You are here to experience the full awareness of life. The great essential for this freedom is the correct point of view — the right attitude — the right understanding. You can have this only by living totally in the now, by letting go of the past moment and by not trying to live in the future … by just paying constant attention to the now and selecting choices to adjust to a course of action that more closely fits with the truth of you.

The one thing in this life process that is constant is *life is change*. When you get into a rut, you're afraid to change. You get certain habit patterns going and become like a machine, like the Pavlovian dogs that were trained to respond to a bell, and your whole life becomes a series of responses. It is a program or belief that comes from outer training and may not be the truth of you. That's not living life, that's existing. You're not in the mainstream at all, you're just on the periphery watching everyone else live. If you're in the mainstream, you flow, you feel together, you are centered, and you are in perfect timing. True change comes from transformation of the personality to your individuality which means becoming more of the Real You. Change is really opening up to life!

Time

This moment never was before, never will be again, and the future moment is always coming up. Right now is all you have. Today is the first day of the rest of your life. There is no time on the spiritual, mental, or emotional levels; there is only now. Time exists only on the physical level of your world. How much of the now are you spending in the past? When you do that, you miss something in the moment. You need to become aware of your own nowness because the secret of life is to be — here, now. *Here is where life is, right now. Always.* Anything else is projecting out of now into the past or future, and it puts you out of synchronicity. You are always in your right place, in the right now, in the right way, in the right time for your growth and unfoldment. You are never late for life. You may be late on the job or late for dinner, but you are always in your right place for your next lesson. The robbers of time are the past and the future. Live fully in the *now*. Your most important task is always in the *now*. Keep your focus in the *now*. Decide *now*.

Because you may have been programmed to a timetable that may not accurately reflect the Real You, on a daily basis it is essential to be mindful of your own natural rhythm. As soon as you can, make the necessary adjustments so you can work, play, and rest in your natural energy flow. It eliminates stress and fatigue. Timing within each person is as unique as a fingerprint.

Where am I? The Observer

Where am I? Are my values current in the now? You always know where your thoughts are centered by what's projected in your outer world.

To detect the areas where you need to make changes so you can be more in charge of your life, be a self-observer. Image your invisible self or your awareness standing inside of your body. Observe your mind, your feelings, and physical body. Just observe impersonally without judgement or condemnation. Act like a detective and see where your focus is. Until you can detach from the mind, emotions, and body, to observe, you keep moving about in the same old programs and recycling patterns from generation to generation almost automatically. It is the observer self who allows you to act from your truth rather than reacting to the outer world or your old programming. It is your Spiritual Self, the Real You, that is centered in the Power and Presence, the superconscious, that gives you answers.

Watch yourself experiencing the experience. From that detached position, you can decide from Power and Love and from your true individuality rather than from the personality or your programmed use of the subconscious, which is based on illusion and fear. To evolve, to unfold on the Spiritual path, it's important to listen to your observer self. It keeps you on your true life course.

Look around you and see what's there. People, situations, places, things, including this book, are part of you. The law of attraction brought everything to you in this particular nowness. Perhaps you see something you don't like, and you say to yourself, "That's a part of me! I can't see where it's a part of me because it's so awful and nasty, it can't be me." It still is. It is a part of your atmosphere. Somewhere along the line, you let negative thoughts in that created a negative situation for you. Don't get depressed about it. Examine it and say, "I don't like that. I can change it."

There are three ways to discern an experience when you are observing you and your response — am I neutral? am I having a negative reaction? or am I having a positive reaction?

If you are having a negative reaction, there is still a like pattern in your consciousness that needs to be resolved. Once you have brought something from the subconscious level to the conscious level, you have a better chance of healing that experience. On the conscious level, you can make wiser choices and take the power out of the negative pattern. Positive thoughts can be assumptions, wishes, fantasies about a situation that may not be the reality, so you can be falsely influenced or overly stimulated. It is when you are neutral, not indifferent, to a pattern that you are aware, consciously and subconsciously, that you have resolved the conflict within yourself, and you can now observe it without being a part of its influence. You are free!

Even though you choose and discern, you don't have to *like* everyone and everything, but you can *love* that universal essence within each person, place or thing. From that point of view, you evaluate a person on a whole different level. There is no reason for competing, comparing, or seeking someone's approval. You are unique. There is only one of you! If there is a person in your experience that is negative and doesn't fit your lifestyle, he or she can be released with love, not resentment and hostility. If you think of clearance or release with love, the situation is gone or adjusted. Just like that — easily, lovingly, and gently. "I release you to your True Life Place and you release me to mine." The situation has no power over you.

As you use the techniques discussed in this book, you begin to break through your own doubt barrier, your own fears, and you can live with more freedom. Freedom is what life is all about. You were born to be free. Free to be and become. It may seem like chaos when you are doing your own thing, but when you are doing your right thing, you move in perfect synchronicity with life. You're not responsible for someone else!

When you're in tune with doing your right thing, you are also in tune with Perfect Love. Not a fairy tale fantasy, controlling, possessive love, but an impersonal, powerful love that functions in and through everything. When you connect with the Divine, It is reflected back to you from everyone and everything. So even though the whole world is negative, by staying centered you get the very best from every person or situation. You move beyond negativity into the Universal Harmony and answers!

– Chapter Two –

Your Five Levels

You are an individualized expression of the creative process functioning in the now on five different levels — the spiritual level, the mental level, the emotional level, the physical level, and the social level. Sometimes you function more on one level than another, and many times you totally ignore the spiritual level. It takes involvement at all levels to experience wholeness or a feeling of well-being. It is important to understand all the levels so you can use the tremendous power available from your inner Self. The goal is to live life from within, not programming from the outer world. The inner to the outer, not the outer to the inner. When you were born, you were given an instrument to use while on planet earth. That instrument consists of the body, the emotions, and the mind. You have a body, but you are more than just a body. You have emotions, but you are more than emotions. You have a mind, but you are more than mind. Let's take a closer look at the five levels.

The Spiritual Level

The spiritual level is the Real You. The spiritual essence of you is who you really are — without beginning and without end as life eternal, infinite, forever. You came into the human experience through birth and will leave through death. On this level, you have everything you need to be and become, and enjoy the journey on earth. You are already perfect. The spiritual level that is within you is beyond dogma, reason, and language. Life Force or

– Figure 1 –

– Figure 1 –

YOUR FIVE LEVELS OUTLINE

NOW

| SPIRITUAL LEVEL | = THE REAL YOU |

| MENTAL LEVEL
EMOTIONAL LEVEL
PHYSICAL LEVEL | = EQUIPMENT |

| SOCIAL LEVEL | = RESULT |

– Figure 2 –

YOUR FIVE LEVELS DETAILED

<u>NOW</u>

YOU ARE A SPIRITUAL BEING
ALL POWER, ALL PATTERN

FUNCTIONS AS DIVINE ORDER,
BALANCE, RHYTHM, HARMONY

INNER LIFE

MENTAL LEVEL = THOUGHT
INITIATES ACTION, GIVES DIRECTION

EMOTIONAL LEVEL = FEELING
INTENSIFIES POWER

PHYSICAL LEVEL = FIVE SENSES
SIGHT, HEARING, TOUCH, TASTE, SMELL.
THE VEHICLE, THE INSTRUMENT

PROCESS EQUIPMENT

SOCIAL LEVEL = RESULT
MAGNETIC LAW OF ATTRACTION;
RELATIONSHIP OF PERSON, PLACE OR THING
FROM USE OF POWER

OUTER LIFE

Spirit or Energy is really God-force. It gives life meaning and purpose. You have all the Power and Patterns beyond anything you could imagine (You brought them here with you.) It is up to you to become aware of the Power and use It to bring forth this essence of life ever-evolving, easily, lovingly, and gently.

The spiritual level contains the patterns of perfection that you came here to express. Since they aren't set patterns, you can choose how this perfection is revealed in your life. You are a totally self-contained unit. You're not like the acorn that still needs the creative soil. Your mind is the creative soil. So you have come into this universe totally prepared. You have the answers within you! It is up to you to choose to reveal them, to accept them. You are connected on the spiritual level to the Universal Intelligence.

Your Inner Power knows all, is everywhere-present, is always available, all-wise, and has all the answers. It is the Universal Intelligence itself, and you are a focal point of it. On the spiritual level, everyone is born equal in the availability of and the of use of this Power. It doesn't appear to be that way because this Universal Intelligence is not being used by everyone at the same level. You are using It at the level of your acceptance. The Power functions through you as desire and intuition or direct knowing.

You are more than your five senses. There's always something within saying, "There's more." When you get tired of all the physical things and say, "Is this all there is?", there is something deep within that says, "No. There is always more."

The Mental Level

The mental level is the steering mechanism of your instrument. Thoughts and words give direction to the Life Energy within you every time you send a command to the Divine Intelligence to produce something. Your life now is a result of your thoughts, words, and attitudes. Thoughts manifest as things! Change your thinking and change your life! What you concentrate on becomes more. What you give your attention is energized. It is not the things you are thinking that make the difference but what you believe. Negative thoughts produce negative results. Focus on what is wrong and you create more of it. Focus on what is right and you become more of what it is. When you control your mind — when you are making choices that are consistent with your nature and that are truly yours — you control your life. Mind is the connecting link between the invisible and the visible.

Your mind is what you have going for you, for it is here that you have choice. Anytime your mind is out of control, you've given up choice of your space. And you're the victim of whatever you are reacting to! So be in control of your mind. Once you connect with the spiritual energy of the universe, you're in constant joy — not overstimulated, but you key into the essence of life, which is harmonious. You don't miss a beat, even the negative experiences have a silver lining!

This is not guaranteeing that your life is a rose garden because life still happens. It is your attitude towards life that is different. Life will never throw you off balance when you stay detached. You may yell and scream, but there will be a part of you that's in control and centered. You know what you're doing. You can act upon your desires, and they'll lift you. The only limitation in the universe is your own limitation. There is no *big* or *little* or *hard* or *easy* — only your thinking makes it so for you.

Mental Exercises

Here are exercises to experience this level of being.

1. Close your eyes and go to a beach in Hawaii. Enjoy the surf. Smell it, feel it, listen to it. Now bring yourself back to the present. Open your eyes.

This demonstrates to you that on the mental level, you can go to Hawaii in a flash in thought. There is no time involved, no space involved. There is also no big or little, hard or easy; there are just your beliefs about them. This opens up a whole new area of experiencing life.

2. Close your eyes again and think about your nose without touching it. Do you know exactly where it is? How about your

ears? Do you know exactly where your skin begins and ends? Open your eyes.

Without touching or seeing your eyes and ears, it isn't definite that they are there. You have an idea that they are there. This demonstrates that you are much more than the body, more than the perimeter of your body. You are able to move and have your being in different areas, different time spans, different dimensions. You can go anywhere in your mind. Are you using this area to its fullest potential?

What the mind can conceive is what the mind can achieve. What you're imaging in your mind is what you're getting in the outer experience. To image in mind is a command to the Power to produce. So check your mental images to make sure that you're picturing what you want to experience. Since there is no time and space on the mental level, whatever you accept subconsciously and consciously produces instantly.

Time is being eliminated, even on the physical level. Consider how long it took the pioneers to travel across the United States in covered wagons. It was months. Then the steam engine was invented, and it took weeks to make the same trip. Later, the airplane cut the same route down to days, and finally the jet down to hours. The trip is no longer recorded in miles, it is recorded in hours. When you speak of going someplace, don't you speak of hours rather than in miles? When you do, you're actually shrinking time on the physical level.

Time, then, only relates to one part of your being — the physical level only. This is why on the mental level it is important to be in the now because that's your valid place — no past, no future, no space, no limitations. Now is all there is!

3. Again, close your eyes and image a dog. Image whatever kind of dog that has meaning or is familiar to you. You draw upon your own mental experience, your own mental attitude, to interpret what is being imaged. Was the dog big or little? Was it a specific breed or a mixed breed? What color was it? Your image was a personal interpretation of what's in your mental atmosphere. You see the world in your unique way.

What that reveals is that you only see your interpretation of the world. This is true of everyone! There is only one person in your universe, and everything is like a mirror reflecting back to you your own consciousness. *What's around you is you.* This includes both physical environments as well as concepts. The word "love" has as many interpretations in this world as there are people. "Peace" has a different meaning to each individual. You are constantly reacting to your own mental atmosphere.

The Emotional Level

Divine Energy flows around you, through you, as you; thoughts flow through your mind, and feelings flow through your body. You feel out of balance when that flow is blocked or impeded, and this creates discomfort in your body. When you attach a thought to a feeling, you are labeling, describing, defining, interpreting, qualifying, or judging, which creates the emotions.

The emotional level adds power and dynamics to thought. Emotion intensifies the thought. When you feel or get emotional, the body is the first to get the charge. It carries the load, and then it reacts. Emotions are programmed from without (man-made), while feelings are natural and come from within. An emotion is an attachment of thought to a feeling. Emotions must never make the choice for you. You do not repress feelings and emotions, but you examine them within your space and then bring them to the mental level to make a choice. If you allow the emotions to choose, you are reacting instead of acting. A reaction is a response to an outer pressure and makes you a victim of the conditions around you. When you bring a problem to the mental level and decide, you are exercising your right to choose, and you are master of the situation — even if you express it in an emotional way. Emotions and feelings are a vital part of the system, but must never dominate the consciousness.

Feelings are not subject to understanding. They just are! Like colors on an artist's canvas, one color isn't more beautiful, more meaningful, or better than another. They are just colors. When they occur together, each provides contrast for the others, and the variety creates interest.

One feeling is no better than another. When you perceive them as having different values and judge them, you impede their free flow and create an energy block. When you define, judge, or interpret feelings about events in your life, you create energy blocks in your body. If you allow the feelings to flow through your body without evaluating, judging, or interpreting them, they can be a most valuable lesson. Any experience you have that is less than perfect is an illusion. By treating it as real, you keep it alive. Judging or interpreting a feeling is an example of keeping an illusion alive, for a feeling is not subject to understanding or definition. It just is. As you cease describing and interpreting it, you let it flow freely through you and allow the true state of your being to come forth.

What is the absence of emotion? It is joyfulness. That is your natural state. The experience of thoughts and feelings against the backdrop or context of joyfulness puts everything in its true perspective and brings you into alignment with the Real You. If you allow yourself to believe in your own perfection and all that flows from it, you open yourself to a constant experience of your natural state, joyfulness. This is the way you express your perfection. Be grateful for the incredible gift that has been given to you to discover and enjoy.

An emotional love is an attitude about another person or object or place. It is inclined to be possessive, it has expectations and generally has an agenda. This is not real love. Real love is Spiritual love that is impersonal, has no agenda, no labels, no attitudes, and it operates in total freedom. It is unconditional!

You are Number One in your space. If you don't like you, why should anyone else? If you don't love you, you can't love anyone else. You can only love another person to the degree that you understand and love yourself. You can't even give love. You can only give the results of yourself experiencing love.

Much of what is labeled love isn't love. It's possession. For example when people get married and one takes control of the other and says, "You just stay on your little pedestal and do what I tell you, then I will love you. If you clean the house, work and cook, and if you're truly obedient, I'll love you forever." That's a bargain. It's not love, it's possession. It is conditional love. It is not loving you for who you are, but loving you for what you do!

True Love, unconditional love, loves enough to let go. True Love trusts *self* totally in the relationship. *Trust yourself!* It is not relevant to trust what someone else says or does. You only have to trust the spiritual energy in the relationship to reveal to you what you need to know to stay in a healthy place. This doesn't mean martyrdom. Martyrdom is love in reverse where you have given your all at a sacrifice. You love to the extent that you're too compassionate and let people tramp all over you. That's not love, that's ego emotion. When you think you are the only one who can do anything to help, you burn out, and then there are two needy people.

Get your emotions under control so you can experience constructive feelings. Feelings that are true to your nature — creativity, joy, happiness, accomplishment, oneness. Fear, hate, resentment, hostility, anxiety, and guilt are not a part of your natural process; they are a part of the subconscious thought of the human race.

Guilt has a tremendous effect on you. Guilt comes from the past. The past programming can cause you to feel guilty about the future. If you give up the past and the future right now in this moment, you can give up guilt. It's simple, but it's not easy. Stay in the now! Give up blame, shame, and guilt forever.

The Physical Level

The physical level is the body which is an instrument that monitors where you are through the five senses — touch, taste, sight, hearing, and smell. It constantly reflects your growth and unfoldment on your life journey on earth. Certainly you are aware of the body. You have to clothe it, feed it, exercise it. It seems to take a lot of time and a lot of money. In the process of growing and maturing, perhaps the physical world is all you're caught up in for a while. You sleep, eat, drink, and be merry until finally you get your body out of balance, and your pleasure becomes your pain. All of those things that you took into your five senses that amused and stimulated you no longer get the job done. A person who stays on this level and doesn't change often ends up as an alcoholic, a drug addict, is suicidal, is depressed by aging or almost any change. You can get to a point where you say, "Gee, dishes again this morning. Another bed to make. What's the use? What's the reason behind all this?" Life can lose its savor and can lose its sense of purpose if the body is allowed to control your life.

You can't function on planet earth without the body. When you get rid of the body, you're in another dimension. You need a body, but you are more than the body. If you absorb anxiety and tension, the body becomes ill and can't function properly. It is vital for health that you are relaxed into the proper tension for the task at hand. The Divine Energy never forces Itself upon you. When your body is blocked by stress, it is cutting off your source of power. The body is like your car. If you drive your car with only a couple of spark plugs sparking, a dirty carburetor, and thick gunky oil, it may run, but it will be sluggish because it isn't in tune. If the body is full of tension, anxiety, and stress, it's not going to perform normally. In order for the body to function properly, it has to be relaxed, free of tension, free of anxiety, and rested.

To connect with that Divine Energy, you have to relax your body. If the body is uptight and stressed, you block that Power and Presence within. The body must be relaxed into peace to allow that Divine Energy to flow. When you find yourself feeling tense, you can use the following relaxing exercise to move you to a point of relaxation (not a trance) so you can flow with events in your life. Do it every day for a minimum of five minutes; ten or fifteen minutes, if you can.

Relaxation Exercise

Do this exercise in a seated position because lying down is almost an instant command to the body to go to sleep. The cross-legged lotus position is fine, but the most important thing is that you are in a comfortable position for you to talk to your body and to get in touch with the deeper levels of your being.

You take control of your body with the mind. Since the mental level is the level that directs your energy, the mind is able to command the body and have the body respond. This takes some training because, until now, the body has controlled you through its own demands of eating, sleeping, drinking, and so on.

Towards the end of the exercise, you build yourself a room in which you can go to rest. Perhaps after doing this exercise for two or three weeks, you won't have to go through the whole process each time. You will become aware when the body has tensed up, and you take care of it right away because it blocks your use of the Higher Power. At that point, all you have to say is, "Body, relax." It does, and you find you have less fatigue. You are more efficient and more effective in your work. You won't have high and low periods because you are continually keeping a balanced flow of Divine Energy coming in. This also prepares you for meditation, which is a listening attitude where you are listening to the silence. But that cannot happen until the body is relaxed. Your body is an energy system. It's similar to an electrical transformer which takes in electricity then diverts it in the proper amperage through the wires of a building to each light fixture and each appliance. If it didn't, electricity would flow in such a large amount that it would blow all the circuits. It's the same with you, so it's important to get your body relaxed and balanced so you can take in this Pure Intelligence, this Divine Energy.

Use an "I" message when you go through the exercise. Sometimes in groups, people help you relax by using a "you" message, for example, "You will relax at the sound of my voice." This is hypnosis. It's an outer control over your space. You're trying to dehypnotize yourself from voices from the past that are still trying to tell you how to live your life. You are always in control when you say "I" or "I am". "I am" is the name of your Higher Self, so there's a lot of power in that phrase.

As you go through this exercise, say to yourself, "I am now in control of my body." Then work with each part of the body. Think about that part, then command it to relax.

To begin the exercise close your eyes. Take slow, deep breaths to help you shift from the outer world distractions and to move your focus inward. Inhale through your nose, hold it a moment, then exhale through your mouth as you release and let go of all negativity, all confusion, all hurrying, all strain, and all worry. Let it go. Breathe in love, intelligence, order, balance, harmony. Then let go. Tense up and relax all of the body. It is surrendering to the Inner Presence, the healing power, a letting go of the outer program.

Start with the toes. Become aware of your toes. Tighten them. Command them to relax. Go to your ankles and be aware of your feet. Tighten them. Command them to relax. Move to your calves. Tighten them. Command them to relax. Move to your knees. Tighten them. Command them to relax. Take a deep breath and blow it out. Be aware of your thigh muscles. Tighten them. Command them to relax. Think about the abdomen. Tighten the stomach muscles. Command them to relax. Move to your hands. Spread your fingers out and tighten them. Command them to relax. Make a fist with your hands. Tighten them. Command them to relax. Slowly move them in a fist again. As you relax, feel the tension leaving the hands. Open and close your hands until you feel all the tension release. Stretch out your arms, tighten. Think of the forearm, then your upper arm. Bend it. Relax. And let your arms drop. Tighten them. Command them to relax. Feel the tension and let it go as you let your arms hang loosely. Place your hands on your thighs. Move to your shoulders. Roll them, forward and raise them up to your ears. Roll them back, and try to let the shoulder blades touch. Tighten them and feel that tension. Gently let go and repeat rolling your shoulders about five times. Again let them go. Inhale and think about all of your organs. Your heart, your stomach, your lungs, your liver. Command them to relax. Inhale deeply and release completely.

Now bring your hands to the back of your neck and gently massage it, then relax. Roll your head from side to side, dropping the chin, and release all the tension in that area. Let it go. Move to your tongue. Think of it and your throat muscles. Command them to relax. Think about the facial nerve centers, around the bottom of the nose, the corners of the eyes, around the ears, forehead. Be aware of facial muscles. Command them to relax. Move to the eye area. So let the eye muscles relax and let go of tension. Say to yourself, "I am now in control. I command my whole body to release, to relax."

Now say to yourself, "I'm moving deeper and deeper into the center of myself. Relaxing, surrendering to the Power and Presence within." Command your mind to be still. Listen to the quiet, the solitude, and rest there.

While you're resting in the silence, build yourself a secret place where only you can come to revitalize, to reenergize, to find answers, to find courage, to find poise, peace, and love. When all else seems to have failed, it's all here for you. You can come here anytime, anywhere. Fill yourself with all the healing, loving energy. All the answers infuse your being. All is well. Rest and be refreshed.

To end this relaxation exercise, take a deep breath, and slowly open your eyes. Become aware of your surroundings. Now you have your body under the control of your mind, and you have a place to go to heal, balance, and rest from the outer world.

The Social Level

The social level is a result of how you have been using your mind, emotions, and body. If you want to check out where your thoughts and emotions are, look around you. Every person, place, and thing in your life is a reflection of your consciousness. Your outer world is always telling you how you are doing. It is a mirror reflecting exactly where you are in your growth and unfoldment. If you don't like what is going on in your life, which your own thoughts created, you can change your choices and your thoughts to change those conditions around you. The greatest gift you can give on this level is to give you back to yourself; and when you have accomplished that in every thought and deed, give everyone back to themselves in thoughts and action.

This helps all your relationships — at home, at work, at play. As you draw upon more of your spiritual nature and bring it into your experience, people who come around you experience more of this love, more of this tremendous Power moving through you; and they feel better just by being in your presence. You prosper! Your world is a joy.

Socially, when you're in the company of another, you're not just communicating on the verbal level; there are other elements of consciousness. On the emotional level, you're having an emotional response to that situation. On the mental level, you are telepathically communicating as well. You have other thoughts. You have thoughts about the conversation, about yourself, about those around you. You are getting a silent secondary message. It can cause confusion in a message being delivered verbally. On the subconscious level, if you stay detached and listen to that particular situation, you intuitively always know the truth.

You are constantly communicating. On the spiritual level, your communication is good everywhere, centered in everything. There are no language barriers on the spiritual level. Spirit is beyond language. There is an infusion of perfect understanding. Everyone is one, there is no "other." When you recognize the Divine in everyone and everything, there are no barriers or misunderstanding, only peace, love, harmony. There is perfect joy, beauty, and good on this level. You can live this truth right now.

Socially you are experiencing all these different levels — physical, emotional, mental, spiritual — with emphasis on the one on which you are centered. For example, if you're centered on the mental level, that will be the dominant communication.

By accepting your divinity and the total Power, you amplify the power of Good and Love in everyone and everything around you. Is it not true that you like to be around those people that love you enough to see through your negative attitudes, your weak points, your fears, and your failures? And they still love you in spite of all you have done to them, like the relationship between a mother and child. Your attitude on this level is one of inclusion, not exclusion.

Because of your personal love, sometimes relationships get out of balance and you become a target. Because that person knows that you love them that deeply, they discharge negativity on you. They know that no matter what they do, you'll love them anyway. Once you become aware of this process and become an observer of yourself, you know when you are taking on their psychic energy and being depleted by it.

Take back your power! Take control of the draining energy that you have given away — maybe to mother, to father, to society. Think *your* thoughts! Establish healthy boundaries. Get centered again.

What kinds of messages are you sending out? What's radiating from you to all your relationships? To uncover the answers, take a look at the people who are in your life now and how you're relating to them. In the silence of your mind you can begin to change the depleting patterns of behavior to those that are higher and better and best. This has nothing to do with liking them. You don't have to like anyone, but you can love the life essence, the Spiritual Presence, within them, without feeling depleted or seeking approval.

A good idea is to make a list of friends, family, and co-workers, and time each person according to the quality of the energy you experience with them. You may have five-minute, one-day, one-week friends, around you before the energy deteriorates. When it does this, say good-bye, excuse yourself, get on with your life! If you don't, you are wasting your time and theirs!

Power

When you succeed in getting detached and observe yourself, you begin to realize that there is something deeper within you. When you finally wake up to this inner Power, It responds to you by corresponding to your thoughts and words. To use this Power that is working all the time at the level of your acceptance, you personalize it by words and thoughts. The Power within you and all about you is inactive in you until you think of It and know that It exists; then you see it flowing from you in limitless measure. It always functions in perfect order, perfect balance, perfect timing, perfect harmony in the now, on your negative thoughts as well as your positive thoughts. It doesn't care. It doesn't argue back. It says yes to everything. It's impersonal. You personalize it.

This Power can be likened to electricity. Electricity has always existed, and it took a man like Benjamin Franklin to have enough courage to question and experiment with it and put some controls on it. Even though you don't understand electricity, you know that if you use electricity with wisdom, you can produce light, cooling, heating, and all sorts of things. You can use the same electrical energy with ignorance and it will kill you.

This is the same principle used with the laws of Divine Mind. It knows only to do. It does not discern, deduct, or say, "You're being a bad person." It is neutral. You give it something to do and it does it at the level of your acceptance. This Power moves through you as you. Use it with wisdom and understanding. *More creates more.* The more you become aware of it, the more you have to use.

The Spiritual part of you always functions when you are relaxed into the proper tension for the task at hand. When you are tense, up tight, anxious, and afraid, you shut the Power off. Just like your car when it's spark plugs aren't working, you're not using full power. When you're moving around, thinking, and doing, and unaware of the kind of an energy system you are, it's a hit-and-miss affair. Turn to the Power within, and It directs you to right action in your experience now. It guides you to answers for the problems that you are facing at that particular moment.

By constantly contemplating, praising, blessing, and giving thanks to this Power, you increase its flow; and as you do this, The Power becomes more potent in your life and more readily accessible to you.

If your channel is cluttered with negativity like many of the channels that are on television today, that's what will be revealed in your outer life. If you look at conversations or general verbalizations, you will find that man speaks in negatives — "You can't do this. This is a horrible day. Oh, it's too hot. I don't feel good." It's the "ain't it awful" syndrome. Many people are more comfortable speaking in that manner rather than saying, "I think it's fantastic! You can do it. This is wonderful!"

So take a look at incoming thoughts, train yourself to say, "Stop. No way. That's not part of the natural flow. I don't accept that.

I have a choice. I take control of my space and turn to the Spiritual Power within me. I may not understand how the Spiritual Power works, but I know it is there and does work."

Because of the *law of attraction, you magnetically attract to you what you are.* This Power and Presence within you is constantly radiating an invisible energy, and through the law of attraction, is drawing to you what you are thinking and feeling. If you are living just on the physical, emotional, and mental levels, you are going to express an emptiness on the social level or in your outer life. If you don't like the physical/emotional/mental experience, you can turn within to Spirit for help, the place where all answers come from. You are a totally self-contained unit. *If you have a problem in your outer world, you have an answer within you to solve it. You must choose how you are going to live — from the inner or the outer.*

Momentarily, turn your mind inward and call upon this all-powerful, all-wise Presence. Open yourself up to perfect order, perfect balance, perfect harmony, and perfect timing in the situation. You feel compelled to right action that takes care of everything!

The more you test it and try it and the deeper your belief, the more you experience the Power, and the greater is your success in your outer experience. Finally you move from "I believe" to "I know." This is a fascinating system, and it's something that is always functioning right now, right where you are. So you begin to monitor your thinking on the mental level in the now, knowing that *thoughts are things and like thoughts attract like things.*

Let's say there's some good that you could accept like a new car or a new coat. If you're relaxed and thinking about that which you can accept, you'll set up that Power and you will draw it to you at the level of your acceptance. But if you question and doubt in your mind and think of it in terms of the future or "do I deserve", your good will almost always be there, but never quite. Are you experiencing that now? Perhaps it's an executive position. Are you ready to accept? They keep offering it to you, but it's never made official. It keeps escaping you. You keep thinking, "When I get to be ... " and it never happens because you are accepting sometime in the future. You never get what you deserve. You only get what you can accept!

The same is true with the past. If you're constantly rehashing the past, which is gone forever, it colors your present and blots out your experience in the now. You feel out of focus. You feel isolated. You feel frustrated, helpless, and lonely when you're working in the past.

Think in terms of the now. Accept right now on the mental level whatever good it is you desire. Give thanks for it in the now. Let it go, and take care of the task at hand. You've relaxed about it, you've set up the law of attraction, and done all your homework, and that's all you need to do — get on with the task at hand.

It's just that simple. Right now. Just by recognizing for a moment that Power and Presence within you, you begin to get a better feeling about yourself. You can experience that Divine Perfection within you in degrees every day. And every day begins to get better and better in every way as you move through the process and take care of one minute at a time. It's a beautiful way to live.

When you get totally in the now on all levels, you experience all the good that life has to offer. If you stay in the past or future, you miss so much of the beauty and the joy and the prosperity that is right here and now.

Chapter Three

Spiritual Laws

The Real You, functioning on the five levels, is in the here and now. Everything you do, you gear from now. What you're thinking now, what you're feeling now is determining your future. If you get up in the morning and are feeling negative, and persist in that, then you set up a law of attraction that makes your whole day a negative experience.

The following are some specific laws of Spirit or laws of energy (Figure 3) that you are using on the mental level now.

1. *Thoughts are things*. Words and thoughts give shape and form to your life. Thoughts initiate the direction that the Divine Energy or Intelligence is to take. Like thoughts attract like things. Your thoughts are the tools of your life experience. Whatever you think either about yourself or others is creative. You *are what you think*. All the thoughts that enter your mind are creating your experience.

2. *Change your thinking and change your life*. When you change your thoughts on the subconscious level, you change the forms and experiences in your life. This is how the universal system works. It is not known *how* it works, it is known *that* it does work.

3. *Spiritual law of attraction*. This is a magnetic law of attraction. The magnetic energy is made up of negative and positive polarities. Thoughts set up our magnetic force field, negative or positive, and attract to it experience of that thought as a physical manifestation. An example is an iron magnet. With both positive and negative energy, it attracts to it what it is — iron. When the polarities are in perfect balance, it creates a neutral force field. Spiritual patterns, which are neutral energy, create wholeness,

complete answers, healings, prosperity, and joy. Like attracts like. What is around you is there because you have attracted it to you with your thoughts and actions. To evolve or grow, you must take responsibility for what is happening to you without shame, blame, or guilt. Use your now experience as a stepping stone to growth.

4. *Law of freedom.* The way something comes into your life is the way something stays in your life. When you bond with something or someone, you are bound to them, and you are no longer expressing as an individual. When situations, conditions, experiences come into your life freely, they can flow freely. Everyone was born to be free. To be a healthy, spiritual individual, you must be free. This is a fundamental principle of the universe. It means freedom through structure. You flow through man's laws, bureaucracy, etc. You don't fight the system, you flow through it like water. Detach so you can be involved without diminishing your uniqueness, and choose to do so freely.

5. *Law of reflection.* Like a mirror, life is always reflecting back to you exactly where you are in your consciousness. It is impersonal and reflects to you where your thoughts and emotions are energized on the subconscious level. What is around you is you!

6. *Law of balance.* This divine law concerns your vitality and energy. When Spirit, mind, and body are synchronized, you have the dynamic energy to flow with life to get your tasks done. It eliminates stress and fatigue. The Life Energy itself is limitless, and it is up to you to keep the flow free of tension, worry, doubt, to keep the mind centered on the within and to maintain a healthy body. Meditation is the key to establishing this in your daily routines.

7. *Law of order.* Order in your life establishes prosperity and clarity. Disorder and chaos block and congest the flow of good. Clutter causes confusion and causes distorted decisions. This means order on all five levels. On the spiritual level, deciding on what is your pathway and clearing out discarded or outdated value systems. On the mental level, keep the mind focused on the task at hand rather than scattered thoughts. On the emotional level, realize reactionary behavior and distractions and change them. On the physical level, create order around you, in

your home, car, work, so there is a free flow of energy. Be proactive, rather than reactive. On the social level, release people, groups, situations that cause confusion and waste time.

8. *Law of timing/rhythm.* There is a natural flow or rhythm to the universal process. There is work, rest, and play. The heart is a perfect example of this law, as are the movements of the sun, moon, oceans and tides, night and day. It is important to discover the rhythm of your life. Are you a morning person or a night person? When is your high energy time or low energy time during a twenty-four-hour period? When are you more extroverted or introverted? There is a flow and rhythm to your life that is unique to you. You are always in your right place for your growth and unfoldment. Adjust your life as soon as you can to live, work, and play in this natural flow.

9. *Law of harmony.* This concerns your relationships and how you relate to persons, places, and things. There is a loving, healing energy that permeates the whole universe, and when it is recognized, it harmonizes circumstances and heals. It is the cohesive factor that keeps the universe running in perfect harmony. This is a natural harmony that exists in all of the universal processes.

10. *Law of circulation.* What goes out from you comes back to you multiplied. It is important to send out love, peace, harmony, and have it returned multiplied. When you deny someone their good, that good is denied you.

11. *Law of vacuum.* Nature abhors a vacuum, e.g., when warm air rises, wind rushes in to fill the vacuum. To create room for the new, it is important to release the old.

12. *Law of release.* Anything you have you must be willing to set free or you are imprisoned by what you possess, that includes people, places, and things.

13. *More creates more.* The universe is ever evolving and becoming more of what it is. It is the same with your world. Whatever you are this moment, if you don't change it, becomes more. Negative becomes more negativity. Joy becomes more joy.

14. *What's true on one plane is true on all planes.* As above, so below; as within, so without. A law is a law whether it is on the

visible or on the invisible plane. Laws are neutral — they are just there. The law of gravity is always the law of gravity, but as you get a greater insight into its properties, you get a greater use of the law. For example, the flight of a bird and of a space shuttle are increased knowledge of the same law of gravity.

15. *No one is your enemy, and no one is your friend. Everyone is your teacher.* Everything and everyone around you is energy in form. To think clearly and get to the truth of person, place, or thing, it is necessary to get rid of labels, bondage attitudes, judgements, opinions, and criticism, and see everything as energy.

16. *Faith is a definite mental attitude which refuses to accept the opposite.* You gain something from everything you pass through; and every event, however adverse, simply tends to arouse more and more of the real greatness within you! You are already living by faith, even though you may not be aware of it. We humans are existing in this energy system, and even with all our goof-ups we're still existing because we have a deep abiding desire to survive and thrive. You really determine your own end every day by words and thoughts. You are either creating a greater life or stagnation.

17. *Everything in the universe came from the invisible before it became visible.* There's an invisible cause that creates a visible effect. What you're learning to do now is to establish true invisible causes so you get a true visible effect. You give to the Power what you want, and with a single-minded focus, you keep your mind on the complete image. If other thoughts persist, just bring the mind back to the complete picture.

Like the camera, the conscious mind gives you the picture. You focus in on it, snap the picture, then turn it over to the Power of the camera, your subconscious mind. Once the subconscious mind accepts it (after you have moved beyond the doubt barrier and your false beliefs), you will experience it. That's all there is to it. The time and space involved is your belief about time and space.

18. *Decide to decide or decide not to decide.* This frees up the energy to flow and prevents congestion and blocking. Spirit does not choose for you; that is your responsibility in life. Once

the choice is made, the energy is directed and must act upon the decision.

19. *Two things cannot occupy the same place at the same time.* If your mind is filled with negativity, there is no room for love. If a cup is filled with water, it cannot be filled with milk. Hate cannot be in the same place as harmony, as light and darkness cannot be in the same place at the same time.

20. *Nothing is ever lost; it is only misplaced.* The subconscious mind is everywhere present. Everyone uses the same subconscious. Like a computer, it stores everything and knows exactly where and what you are looking for; and it can reveal it to you if you stay calm, relaxed, and allow the answer to come to you. You never lose anything that belongs to you. There may be times when you feel you've lost someone you love because he or she has moved out of your life. If that person belongs in your life, he or she won't go away. They may move out for a while until things get back in balance, and as soon as that is accomplished, they will move back into your life, in harmony and peace.

21. *What you concentrate on, you become.* If you focus on the problem, you increase the problem. If you concentrate on the answer, you get the answer.

22. *What you identify with, you become.* What you don't say no to, you're saying yes to. Exercise your choice. If you are not choosing, something or someone is choosing for you!

23. *Where attention goes, energy flows.* When your mind dwells on anything, it energizes the experience.

24. *What you resist, you give power to.* The way of this life path is nonresistance. You flow rather than force. Be like water — it takes the shape of whatever vessel it is in. Water takes the course of least resistance, but does not lose its integrity. It is always water. This doesn't mean you let yourself be walked upon or that you are believing that everything is doing well when it isn't. You accept where you are right now, and you know there is something better. You lift yourself into a higher vibration or higher frequency of good. So you don't resist negativity. Any resistance is negative! You see through it. You move beyond the fact and the appearance to the truth. Whatever the experience or

condition is outside of you, once you see through it, you can control it, you dissipate it, and bring forth your true life answer!

25. *Life flows from the inner to the outer.* The plant comes from the seed; the chicken comes from the egg; and a baby comes from the womb.

26. *Operate from principle, not personality.* Personality is stored knowledge of the mind and emotions. It carries a great deal of misinformation. It is also duality — good/bad — fragmented information. Principles come from the divine laws or natural laws of the universe and are consistent in the flow of life. When you use these laws, you align yourself with oneness (how the law always works). Use of these laws creates definite results.

27. *Principle is not set by precedent.* Just because things have been done a certain way doesn't mean it's the right way for you. When Columbus left to sail the ocean blue, he was told he was going to fall off into a pit of dragons. Many concepts, like the earth is flat, are false concepts. Find a new way to do the same old thing. If the law of gravity was complacently accepted, humans would have never flown. Someone got inspired from the spiritual level and that guided the mental level to develop a mechanism (the airplane) by which humans can fly. When you hit a stalemate, get relaxed and go within. Let your inner Self lead you and guide you into a new insight to the solution.

28. *Now is all there is. You are in the right place, at the right time, in the right way for your growth and unfoldment.* You may be late for work or lunch, but you're never late for life. Be aware, pay attention to what's going on now!

29. *Energy and matter are equally interchangeable. All they do is change form.* Ice becomes water becomes steam becomes water becomes ice.

30. *Do the thing, the Power is there.* There is a natural harmony that is true within everyone. You have certain needs, and if you make a decision to do the thing, the Power is there now. In other words, if you have a desire to do something, take the first step by deciding to do it, and the universe supports you all the way.

Don't wait until everything is perfect. If you want to do an oil painting, do it. Many desire to paint, they go out and buy the brushes, oils and canvas, then they're afraid to paint the first stroke because it may not be a Monet. Go ahead and paint and get your failures out of the way!

The most important part of anything is taking the first step. With any task or idea you have, use the courage in the now to make a commitment to yourself. Give yourself permission to take that first step, then watch life bring you the people you need, the finances you need, the ideas you need. It'll all come flowing if you stay relaxed in the here and now and accept it.

31. *Move in action, not reaction.* Are you acting or reacting? This pertains to attitudes and adjustability. When you live on just the physical and emotional and the mental levels, you're reacting to information that is coming in through your five senses and you're trying to make sense out of it. Again, you're out of control because you're not making the decisions. Someone else is. You are deciding from the outside information.

That's why it's important to recognize your automatic patterns that cause you to respond. It is important to stop and think and decide if it is what the Real You wants to do! You may opt to operate in that old pattern, but there's a difference. You are opting to do it because you chose to. That is power!

32. *The higher use of the law controls the lower use of the law.* This is a premise that works on all levels, whether it's physical energy or emotional energy or mental energy. Basically, the reference here is mental energy. The higher (positive) use of language, words, and thoughts will always control the negative (lower). How many of your words and thoughts are spent in the negative or the positive? The problem or the answer? The higher thought is more powerful than the lower thought.

At times when all obvious conditions are saying life is awful and things are worse than ever, by using an affirmation like, "I am better today in every way," you are using a higher thought and the negative has to move out. What you've told the situation is you don't accept the appearances, for you know you are to live a life of joy and prosperity and peace and answers. Spirit leads mind; mind leads emotions, which then act upon the body.

33. *High energy flows to low energy.* A high energy person uplifts and energizes the low energy person.

34. *What your mind can conceive, you can achieve.* In other words, what you can put into words and thoughts or picture in your mind, you can achieve at the level of your acceptance. The beautiful part is Spirit will lead you. You'll get one idea, and if you relax and ponder on it, you'll begin to follow that idea with another idea until soon you have the complete picture or answer.

When it's done in mind, it's very easy to act upon it. Like building a house. First the architect gets the idea. Spirit supplies the inspiration, mentally the architect accepts the idea, and then physically acts upon it and puts it on paper as a blueprint. The blueprint is given to a contractor who builds the house. And it is done from the Invisible to the visible. You're a three-dimensional being, you are spirit, mind, and body, evolving to the fourth dimension of enlightenment.

35. *The law is inclusive, not exclusive.* The universal system includes everything. It does not select, argue, or deduct. Its purpose is to unite not to divide, to include not to exclude, to accept not renounce.

36. *Detach so you can be involved.* This means giving up attitudes, opinions, judgements, criticism. It means watching or witnessing what the mind, the emotions, and the body are doing and deciding on action. Then the spiritual Self, the Real You, is in charge of directing your consciousness. You move from the personal to the impersonal unconditional love.

37. *If you fail to control your own mind, you can be sure you can control nothing else.* Since mind is the gateway, if you've given over the control of your mind to someone else, you've given up your birthright. You're giving up your right to be. Your freedom exists where your integrity exists — your right to choose on all levels. It isn't just the obvious choice, it is, "What is true for me? What is real for me?"

What is true right now is right for you, regardless of whether it's right for society or not. Control your own mind and see which of your patterns are repeating over and over. The reasons behind those old patterns are sometimes so obscure, it's very difficult to find their roots. For example, a child was watching her mother cook the ham for Easter dinner. The mother cut off each end of the ham and put it in a pan, then the oven. The child asked why the ends were cut off, and the mother replied, "That's the way Grandma always did it." Later, Grandma came to dinner, and the child asked her, "Why did you cut off the ends of the ham?" The grandmother answered, "Because the pan I used was too small."

38. *Definite plans bring definite results.* Scattered thinking with no direction creates chaos. If you don't know where you are going, how do you know when you get there?

– Figure 3 –

SPIRITUAL LAWS

1. Thoughts are things.
2. Change your thinking and change your life.
3. Law of attraction.
4. Law of freedom.
5. Law of reflection.
6. Law of balance.
7. Law of order.
8. Law of timing/rhythm.
9. Law of harmony.
10. Law of circulation.
11. Law of vacuum.
12. Law of release.
13. More creates more.
14. What's true on one plane is true on all planes.
15. No one is your enemy, and no one is your friend. Everyone is your teacher.
16. Faith is a definite mental attitude which refuses to accept the opposite.
17. Everything in the universe came from the invisible before it became visible.
18. Decide to decide or decide not to decide.
19. Two things cannot occupy the same place at the same time.
20. Nothing is ever lost; it is only misplaced.
21. What you concentrate on, you become.
22. What you identify with, you become.
23. Where attention goes, energy flows.
24. What you resist, you give power to.
25. Life flows from the inner to the outer.
26. Operate from principle, not personality.
27. Principle is not set by precedent.
28. Now is all there is. You are in the right place, at the right time, in the right way for your growth and unfoldment.
29. Energy and matter are equally interchangeable. All they do is change form.
30. Do the thing, the Power is there.
31. Move in action, not reaction.
32. The higher use of the law controls the lower use of the law.
33. High energy flows to low energy.
34. What your mind can conceive, you can achieve.
35. The law is inclusive, not exclusive.
36. Detach so you can be involved.
37. If you fail to control your mind, you can be sure you control nothing else.
38. Definite plans bring definite results.

Chapter Four

Premises to Ponder

What is in your whole mental atmosphere? It is the conscious, subconscious, and superconscious minds. What can you do to use this knowledge effectively?

Look at the expansiveness of mind. You are immersed in a sea of Mind or in a sea of Intelligence or Life Energy (Mind, Light, Spirit each means God Power), like the fish in the sea are immersed in salt water. Fish are not aware of the medium or the substance they're in, they just function in it and accept it. The same is true for you.

Conscious, Subconscious, Superconscious Levels

This Mind stuff is impersonal and doesn't care what it does. You personalize it with your words and your thoughts. It is impersonal, it's inexhaustible, and it's limitless. It doesn't hold back by saying you can only have so much and that's all for you, it lets you have as much as you can accept. You're using it all the time on three levels — the conscious mind, the subconscious mind, and the superconscious mind. (Figure 4)

Conscious Mind

The *conscious mind* is your awake time, when you can make your choices. It functions when you wake up in the morning until you go to sleep. You know who you are and where you are. Upon waking, you begin to function and to make decisions. This mind

– Figure 4 –

MENTAL LEVEL

Conscious Mind

Awake times — does not operate when you are asleep.

Choice

Doubt Barrier

Personality, outer programming, the ego
(intellect and emotions)
Use of subconscious. Stored knowledge.
Past   –Soul–   Future

Subconscious

Always awake, always says "yes". Doer, medium, law.

Now
Superconscious
Spirit • The Real You
Perfect Patterns • Perfect Power
Awareness, individuality,
intuition.

EXPERIENCE

When conscious and subconscious agree,
you have experience.

functions best when it has a single decision. When you know what you want and you make a decision, this mind functions efficiently and effectively.

If you have two or three thoughts going through your mind, it becomes inefficient and ineffective and almost paralyzes your action until you decide. This doesn't mean that you can't be doing one thing and be thinking about another. This means if you subjectivize a thought and it becomes automatic, like driving a car or riding a bike, you had to think through the step-by-step learning process before it became a subconscious action. Now you do not have to consciously think it through!

The purpose of the conscious mind is to choose, to select what it is you desire to experience. What the conscious mind chooses becomes a command to the subconscious mind to do.

The conscious mind has a definite function, and if you're not selecting the pictures or the thoughts that are being presented to the subconscious mind, someone else is. If you're not doing your programming, television is, the newspaper is, your neighbor is, your family members are, or your society is. If you don't take control of you, you are not expressing your individuality (the reason you entered this life), and you experience comfort only in short moments. If you want to get comfortable, you have to get in touch with the Real You!

The conscious mind can be used like a television. When the thoughts and pictures are coming in, you are busy evaluating them by standing guard at the doorway of your mind. If a negative comes into your mind, you just say, "I do not accept that," and replace it with a higher thought. If you release the negative, creating a vacuum, and you don't chose to replace it with a positive affirmation, something more negative will come in because in nature there is the principle, "nature abhors a vacuum," and nature rushes to fill it with the same vibrational energy, only with more velocity.

It's your responsibility to select carefully with your conscious mind. Thought by thought, word by word, be aware of what's going on in your head. It's your life!

Subconscious Mind

The subconscious mind is the powerhouse. It is the storehouse of all memory. It is energy itself. All humans are immersed in the subconscious mind. Everyone is using the same subconscious mind. That's why some can communicate with others without speaking. In the subconscious mind is where all psychic phenomena or extrasensory perception takes place. There is no time or space on this level. Programming your subconscious mind goes on twenty-four hours a day. The subconscious never sleeps; it says "yes" to everything. When you are not controlling the conscious mind by standing guard at the doorway of your thoughts and choosing what goes into your subconscious, someone or something else from the outside is controlling it. The subconscious is automatically attracting what is energized on this level.

The subconscious mind acts as an engine. It does not deduct; it says yes to everything. It's impersonal. It simply takes what it is given and acts upon it. If you just let any kind of thoughts come in, that's what is produced around you.

Your use of the subconscious mind, to this point, is your development of your ego personality. But you are more than your personality. You are a unique individual that is the Real You, the superconscious. It is important that the superconscious mind, your Spiritual Presence, guides, guards, and compels you into saying the right thing, doing the right thing at the right time and in the right way to be in charge of all your actions. This takes you beyond any outside programs that are active in your subconscious now.

It's not enough in life to experience the storehouse of someone else's program about yourself that you have accepted as true. Maybe an authority figure like your mother, father, minister, or teacher told you things like you were good or bad, an easy child to raise or a hard child to raise, that you're bright or stupid. Whatever you accepted of their image is the image that you believe about yourself, and you project that in your experience.

Perhaps you're not projecting the Real You at all. Maybe you're projecting a potpourri of everyone's thoughts about you.

When that is going on, you never feel together or centered. Instead, you feel a little isolated, frustrated, and anxious. You are fearful. You never feel loved because all you know about love is coming from the outside. When you speak, you always quote what someone else said. "He says, she says, they say" are all outside authorities to validate your thought! Seldom do you say, "I think." When someone isn't there to tell you how great or handsome or beautiful you are, you feel none of those things. Your programming needs to be reexamined to see what truly is you or what is someone else telling you who you should be. When you are being *real*, you are supported by the Divine Presence within you with all the love there is. Praise and criticism from the outside do not affect you either way. You know you are enough.

Superconscious Mind

The superconscious mind consists of the Perfect Patterns and Perfect Power of all the forms in the universe It is all-powerful, all-wise, all-knowing, and everywhere-present. It is impersonal, unconditional love. It is beyond thought, labels, or the roles you play. It is first cause. It is absolute. It has no beginning and no end. It's eternal, infinite, and immeasurable. No boundaries! Its center is everywhere-present and its circumference is unlimited. The superconscious mind is your perfect Self — it is The Real You.

You are a focal point of this creative Intelligence, and the Real You is whole and complete now. You always know when you're being you. That's when you are centered, joyful, peaceful and poised because that's how the superconscious expresses. That's when you know that you know beyond reason or logic. You can always trust your intuitive nature, the inner Self that leads you into what is right action for you while all else may be telling you what is wrong with your life. Only you can know what is right for you. That's why there's no one else quite like you. You are unique. You are an individualized expression of the superconscious, or this Divine Intelligence. That is also why the Real You does not seek approval. By seeking approval you are trying to live up to someone else's standards, which may not be your standards at all.

Living your Real You patterns, the superconscious Patterns of Perfection, and following your inner guidance brings perfect order, perfect balance, perfect timing, and perfect harmony from where you are to where you're going. Those around you cannot control you or drain you. You are magnetic, charismatic, dynamic. People want to be around you because you're a positive, centered person, and the energy that comes from you is automatically uplifting, inspirational, and healing.

Do Your Own Programming

When you feel fearful, unsure of yourself, insecure, and you have a low self-image, that's the image that is projecting from your subconscious mind to someone else's subconscious mind. On the surface, you may look like you have it all together, and you may be impressive with all the physical trappings on the outside, but you send an underlying message of fear. There is something unsettling about you because you're uneasy about yourself. Continuous communication on the subconscious level is always going on.

Take control of your subconscious mind with your conscious mind. Make your own choices. Learn how to let go and release old thoughts that are playing like a tape recorder inside of you, telling you the should's, ought to's, and have to's. In transactional analysis, it is called the "parent tapes" made by the authority figures in your life. Are they still running the show? Is their material valid? Is it updated and meaningful now? Is it the Real You?

When you take over and do your own programming, where you're experiencing fear, you can consciously say to yourself, "There is no fear in the natural universe. That is a programmed thought. I am safe, secure, poised, peaceful. I trust the Divine Presence!" Either in this lifetime or in other lifetimes, all fear is programmed.

Two things cannot occupy the same place at the same time. It's like light and darkness. Darkness is not a thing in itself. Where does it go when the light comes on? Darkness is merely the absence of light. Another example is success and failure. You are always succeeding. You are succeeding at success or succeeding at failure. If you think lack and limitation, you will never have enough. By changing your thought about it and saying, "I live in a universe of abundance. Prosperity is all around me. It is natural, so, therefore, it is my birthright to experience prosperity. I am prosperity." The 'I am prosperity' is the truth. You may be temporarily without funds, but you're not saying you're broke. You identify with the prosperity within, and knowing that if you change your mind about your situation, you change the experience.

A prosperous mind doesn't listen to statistics, it knows there are riches within. A prosperous mind knows that there is good everywhere, and you can have what you can accept. You never get what you deserve. You get what you accept in consciousness.

You are automatically a success if you get your bloated nothingness out of the way of divine circuits. When you let old programming of "it can't be done," "it's impossible," "it won't work," play on, that's what you experience. If you have some of that programming going, stand guard and consciously work with it to change to the creative positive answers. When you're failing, just say to yourself, "I'm a success at failure right now. But I am a success!" It is the same energy, "I can change the direction of my thought and change the direction of my life now."

If you are having problems in some areas, look them over and see what kind of thoughts are holding them in place. For example, sickness and health. All the sickness in the world is not going to make health abnormal. Health is natural. Sickness is the misuse of mind and emotions that acts upon your body. You may ask, "So why do I feel like I do now?" It's because your choices are reflecting poor health. If you decide to have an affair with a germ, you have chosen (sometimes unwittingly) to have that experience.

Colds are a result of indecision or confusion. When you get a cold, look at it. Examine your thoughts and see what you're copping out from. Society, once in a while, puts you in a strange circumstance. Let's say you're working, and suddenly you just can't hack it anymore. You're confused. You feel the need to get away from work and go somewhere to clear your mind. Usually, you can't go to your boss and say, "I've got to go home and get my mind together today." He's likely to say, "Here's your paycheck, and I know the name of a good shrink."

But if you catch a cold and your nose is dripping, your employer may be very glad to pay you to go home and get better. With your cold, you've got your day that you can spend in silence or stay in bed — just get away from the world and get yourself together.

On the other hand, while you're lying in bed with your cold, you get a phone call from someone that says, "You have won a trip around the world. To accept the prize, you must leave at once and fly to Europe. You have to pack your bags right now and leave for the airport." How long would you stay in bed with your cold? Your cold would go immediately!

You can make a difference in the control of your health. The process of healing is the same and has a perfect pattern for healing. The cells go through the same steps of healing, whether you go through it in a minute or a year. Where is your attention centered? Is it centered on developing an illness, or is it centered on getting well?

The conscious mind and the subconscious mind work together to produce your experience. If you give the right command to your subconscious mind, it will produce a life of joy and harmony. When your conscious mind recognizes the superconscious mind, there is a pattern of peace, joy, harmony, and prosperity right now within you and you move past any doubt. Your life is brought into a new dimension of harmony and peace, right now, right here on planet earth — even amid all surrounding negativity.

Your life and lifestyle and the joy you can experience are totally up to you. With your words and your thoughts, what are you choosing for you right now?

With your words and thoughts *in the now,* begin to change those areas that are not bringing to you the joy you can experience. *You are always in the right place, at the right time, in the right way for the level of your growth and unfoldment.*

Exercises

Here are experiments to establish proof that directing your thoughts works. As you go about your daily activities, observe your mind, emotions, and body, and experiment with the following exercises to prove the philosophy to yourself.

Exercise 1 — Green Lights

The first exercise is the green light exercise. First, know that there is only one of you! Therefore, there is only first place, no second place. Right now you are in the right place. Just be. Accept you as you find you. That is the Truth of you. You can have green lights and flow through traffic easily. Turn this thought over to the Higher Power within you, the Real You, and get relaxed. Give the command without meddling, coercing, or forming opinions, and trust the command to take you gently through traffic. Say to yourself, "I am in the right place, in the right time, in the right now, in the right way."

Don't try to outguess the city engineers. That is when you are trying again to meddle, coerce, scheme, and manipulate the law. The law and how it works is a mystery, and it's enough to know that it works. Trust yourself. Manipulating and scheming have boxed you in — it is another form of control. Flow with the activities of life. Express a feeling of oneness with all good everywhere. Within you there is a synchronization that keeps you from bunching up at the light at the same time. State silently, "I now accept this green light easily, gently, and lovingly." If you get relaxed and in tune with yourself, you will flow from green light to green light.

Exercise 2 — Parking Place

Another exercise is done regarding a parking place. Since there is only one of you and you're always in your right place, why should you park in the back of the lot? There's a place right up in front for you. All you have to do is let your mind accept it. The next time you go shopping or to the bank, accept your parking place on the mental level before you leave. Pick your place in your mind, visualize and accept it in the now, command your subconscious mind that you accept it in the right way. You don't have to bang someone's fenders to get in, you accept your space is waiting for you. Then proceed without doubts like asking, "Does this work?" or "Who am I to think I have to be up front?" Some people think they don't deserve it, so they always get second best. There's only first for you, the best in life for you, unless you become a second-best person. Often times, you will have a space chosen and it's taken. Don't start doubting. Affirm, "My parking place is here. I accept it easily, gently, and lovingly." Someone will come running out of the building and pull out right in front of you, and there will be a place for you with money in the meter.

In these exercises, you are not just getting a green light or a parking place. You're using mind, you're telling the Power what you desire, and you're getting it. You're not taking it away from anyone else because if everyone else is doing their right thing, there is a natural flow. It's like every star has its place in the sky. So do you. As you continue to get green lights and parking spaces, you will learn that if you can control those things that you can apply those same principles in other areas in your life.

Exercise 3 — Mirror

A third experiment is an exercise to start off your day. The first thing you do is look in the mirror. Look past the physical and form no opinions or judgements about it. Say, "I am great. I am beautiful (or handsome)." As soon as you say that, you may get an argument, "Who do you think you are?" That's old programming trying to put you down.

You're not saying you are greater than anyone or better than anyone. You're just saying because you breathe in and breathe out, it's a miracle. You are life expressing. That's amazing! And your life is a gift!

Now say to yourself, "I am wonderful." Go past any feedback you may get. You are wonderful because you eat hamburgers and greasy fries, and the results are fingernails and hair. That's awesome! There is a system within you that gives you all these things. You didn't give you to you, and you can't take you away. You can use It (the law of mind) to produce good in your life by choosing.

Now try, "I am a success right now." If you get feedback and arguments from that, just say, "I am better today than I was yesterday."

Try these affirmations to get in touch with the Real You. There's something that you came here to be and become that you can do better than anyone else, something at which you are already successful. That Pattern is there and that Power is there if you choose to align yourself with It.

You are great. You are wonderful. You are a success. Right now.

Chapter Five

Attitudes and Adjustability

Your attitudes are the way you feel about things plus your opinions. Your feelings give power to a thought. You cannot be on the spiritual path and insist on retaining attitudes and behaviors that are not compatible with the way of enlightenment. If you are not willing to make these changes for your growth, you must be content to remain mentally confused and emotionally upset. You can alter your life by altering your attitudes. Keep a relaxed but directed attitude toward everything — relax into peace, into poise, into prosperity, into health, into answers, into right action. Focus on what is right rather than what is wrong. Focus on answers rather than problems.

Attitude Inventory

It is useful to do an attitude inventory about every six months to stay current. In Figure 5, are three lists using the five levels of your being. Working with these five levels can give you surprising insights in changing attitudes and establishing your goals. Get into a relaxed mode so the subconscious mind can reveal where you are.

Prepare an elimination list to help you realize where you need to update your value system and change your negative ways. Change is what life is all about, and if you don't change, you become stagnant — like a pool of standing water.

The elimination list can include old value systems that no longer work as you develop your studies on inner knowing. Perhaps you will find it necessary to change your philosophical

– Figure 5 –

ATTITUDES AND GOALS EVALUATION LIST

To examine attitudes and clarify your goals, evaluate each list from your five levels — physical, emotional, mental, social, and spiritual — to establish where you are NOW.

I eliminate from my life now, easily, lovingly, gently.	I accept my good now, easily, lovingly, gently.	I give thanks for...
I now release worn-out conditions and completed situations to their True Life Place, and they release me to my True Life Place.		

views or your religious beliefs. You want to rid yourself of anything that takes away your self-esteem or power! Mentally, you want to eliminate indecisiveness, seeking approval, and negative images of gloom and doom. Check out authority figures and see where you are giving up control of your life to someone else. Maybe it's time to eliminate some boundaries of lack and limitation, opening the way for prosperity. Where do you need to give yourself permission to grow? or to change? or not to obey? Emotionally, are you letting fear, anger, revenge, resentment, hostility, pride, vanity, or frustration make the decisions? The emotions are the power level and they intensify thoughts; so you must let the mind decide, not the emotions. Emotions create victims when they are allowed to make decisions.

On the physical level, check what is around you, for that is your life mirror revealing what your consciousness at the present moment is manifesting. What do you need to release? Where are you blocked? How about your health? Where is there disorder? Chaos?

Socially, what needs to be released or added to bring more freedom in your life? Do you need to reevaluate your relationships so you only express quality time? For example, five-minute friends or weekend friends. What organizations do you belong to that are no longer contributing to your success? What is creating an imbalance in your times of work, rest, and play? Do you need to give up some TV watching? Sports? Gossiping? How much time do you spend on the telephone? Do you let it interrupt your work, your focus, your concentration? Take charge!

Prepare a second list stating, "I accept" rather than "I want." The law of mind is exact, so if you "want," that is exactly how the law interprets it; and you continue wanting. Give up "need" and "want" and learn to *accept now* your heart's desire. There is no "should," "ought to," or "have to" on the list either. To be effective, it must be what *you* desire, rather than what your children, your family, or society desire. It is not valid if it is not for you! Do not get into the how, that is, how this is going to come about because how the law of mind works is still a mystery. We *know* that it works!

As you make this list, don't limit yourself because of money. Just get down on paper everything you can conceive. At the end of the list, you can review and decide between priority or preference or what is compulsive or addictive.

The third list is for Thanksgiving. It is the most important of all — for it is an attitude of gratitude that increases your acceptance of a healthy, happy consciousness. It eventually will be, by far, the longest list! This list recognizes what you have achieved using the tools revealed to you in this book.

Changing Your Attitudes

Use techniques like visualization to change your attitudes and help move you through the doubt barrier. Make the image one of livingness and of being in the midst of life, rather than standing on the edge feeling fearful and left out.

Think of your subconscious mind, your attitudes or programming, as a flowing river. When you're flowing in synchronization with the True Self, you are flowing in order, balance, rhythm, and harmony, you're in the mainstream and going with life. When you're negating and fighting life by feeling fearful, doubtful, hateful, and resentful, all these things place you in a mud bank. It is like trying to swim upstream. Age has no discrimination here. Even young children can feel so deeply depressed that their lives seem over, a closed book. They shut down and withdraw from life.

Life is energy and has to flow somewhere. If you are directing the energy negatively, it's going to boomerang on you. So you have to keep it moving and radiating outward, then you are free to flow and express creatively. Express, don't repress!

How do you change negatives like fear? With affirmations. When you get negative feedback from stating an affirmation, change it to one that you can handle mentally, like "I am better today in every way," or "I am poise. I am Power. I am courage." Use whatever words you need to change the energy to the positive. "I am love. I am lovable. I am loved." Use a positive affirmation to get rid of the negative.

"I now accept a dramatic change for the better in all of my affairs." With that kind of affirmation, you won't get feedback from the subconscious mind. Whereas, "I am a success" can bring doubts as your mind reminds you of all the failures you had yesterday and the days before. Keep saying the neutralizing affirmations until you're back in the mainstream and flowing with life again.

The ego always tries to keep you under its control. You are really two people. The ego self is all of your programming up to now. It's your lesser self that has had full control. Connect with the Inner Self, the Real You, your Spiritual Self so you can neutralize the programming of the ego, within your subconscious mind. The ego always puts up a struggle. The personality in the subconscious is a bank in which like thoughts band together and accumulate. This is why you can create your own atom bomb that will destroy you — if you hate enough and keep on hating, it will build up to the point of explosion and you are the one who will be destroyed.

More creates more is a natural law. Unless you change your hate to love, it will become more, and eventually it undermines everything you do. You become so overcome with fear and hate that you are paralyzed by it, just as surely as you're breathing.

Fear is the base of all negative thoughts and actions. When you move forward in truth, your fear-based negative attitudes can no longer bog you down or hold you back. As you lighten your load of them, you light up your pathway.

Your Aura

A major technique to control your energy patterns is to study your aura. You have around you several energy fields that are as valid as the physical body. Your aura is normally about two to eighteen inches away from your body. Therefore, when people stand too close to you, they are standing in your space, your aura.

If you look at a room full of people, you can see that most people are comfortable with about eighteen inches to three feet between them and any other persons. However, when two people are communicating and a positive law of attraction is operating, they move in closer to each other and each other's aura. The law of attraction is so strong in some people, they can't let each other go and continue to live in one another's aura.

Energy Fields

Within your aura are different energy fields, (Figure 6) which can be referred to as light bodies that relate to each one of the different levels of your being — mental, physical, emotional, and spiritual. Kirlian photographic equipment can capture on film some of these energy emissions from the body. These are real energy bodies that you need to learn to control to be in charge of your space. When you are aware of this electrochemical magnetic force field, you no longer have to feel sapped or drained, nor do you need to be open and read by someone who is working in the psychic realm unless you want to be. If you can control your force field, you can control incoming and outgoing messages and thoughts.

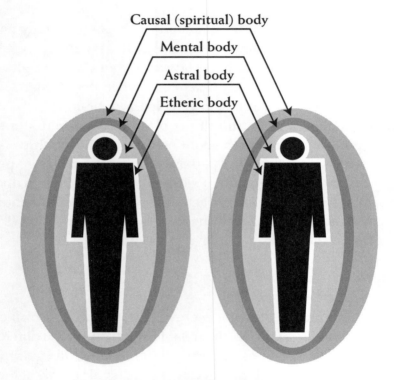

– Figure 6 –

HEALTHY AURA

Causal (spiritual) body

Mental body

Astral body

Etheric body

A healthy communication between two energies.

– Figure 7 –

AURA CONTAMINATION

Contamination between two energies.

Absorption of the other energy.

If someone has control of your mind, they own you.

One of these energy bodies or energy fields is what is called the vital or etheric body, that is the perfect pattern of the physical body. Every part of you, your appendages and your organs, has a perfect pattern of light energy that is circulating in and through your body to sustain it. An example of this is when someone has had a leg amputated. For a period of time after the leg is removed the person can still have feeling in the phantom limb, the area where the leg once was. Knowledge of the etheric body can assist you in healing the body by identifying with this Perfect Pattern of the body.

The next time you cut yourself or bruise yourself, don't react. Identify first with the perfect healing pattern. Before you enter the drama, think about your energy pattern to keep and maintain your physical body at the highest, finest, and best. You can affirm wholeness — "I affirm the Perfect Pattern expressing through me now, healing and revealing the Truth."

Another energy body reflects your emotional level, and it fluctuates according to the way you're feeling. It is called the astral body. If you're feeling great, it expands and radiates from you. If a person is in love or feeling very joyful, you can feel that energy radiating from him or her. If you can see it, it radiates in various colors.

If you're emoting depression, it will set up the law of attraction and bring more of that same emotion into your energy field. Also when you are sad or depressed, the field is muddy and dark and the energy field gets smaller, then you feel confined and restricted.

Around the emotional energy field is the mental energy field that radiates and interpenetrates it. It is activated by thought. When you are being very intellectual, this is the energy field that is activated and receives the energy first. It affects the emotions because the mind leads the emotions, then the mind and emotions together work on the body. So if you're really negative and you back it up with feeling, you're going to end up with something on the body that doesn't belong there, disease!

Around the aura is what is called the causal body that expresses the spiritual level and is energy at its highest and finest.

Within this causal body are the Perfect Patterns and Perfect Power of everything that exists. It is the Real You.

This Divine Energy is what you're trying to connect with and bring into your life to get the benefits mentally, emotionally, and physically. When this causal form is crystallized and balanced with the other energy bodies, you live a life of inspiration and service that is a joy to behold and benefits all of mankind. Acceptance of your divinity brings you into cosmic consciousness where you are one with all of nature and all of life. All of life on this level lives in harmony. When you're full of energy and feeling vital, you're full of Light.

As your awareness of your own energy fields develops, you are able to feel or see energy moving from one person to another in a room. You can feel when a person comes into the room and draws energy from everyone else. When you're around someone and later feel drained, it is because that person came into your force field and borrowed some of your energy. There is no limit to the energy on the spiritual level, but your mind, emotions and body can be affected if you are not in control of your own space. You are constantly in contact with others in this way. Every time you communicate with another, you are exchanging through the subconscious mind. Everything filters though your subconscious mind. Whatever is stored there can be activated. Let's say that someone is yelling at you and really projecting anger. As it is coming to you, you have a choice to make. Are you going to react and let it trigger all of your anger? Or are you going to stop it before it gets into your aura?

You can be aware when someone is directing a negative thought to you from a distance or in your presence. This is true particularly when you've had an intimate relationship and when you have been involved emotionally and mentally. Usually with those you love — children, families, friends — you've opened your space to them. It doesn't help you or the intruder to have this negative energy exchange going on. When this negative energy comes to your force field, you can stop it by choosing the right thought.

Order your body to relax into the proper tension. There are several ways to take control.

Words and thoughts control the force field. Words in the form of an affirmation such as, "I now take charge of my energy field so that only Good comes in and Good goes out," are powerful, and they will dissolve anything that doesn't belong. Let's say that you are having a great day until suddenly you feel your energy being drained by someone entering your force field. Any time anyone projects a group of thoughts to which you are sensitive or vulnerable, it may take persistent use of affirmations to gain and to keep control of your aura. Imagery can also be effective. Image yourself in a cocoon of white light; and then imagine a filter as a window where you choose what enters and what you do not allow entry.

Once your space is under control, you flow in perfect harmony with all of life. With this tool, you can evaluate all the people in your life on this basis. Make a list of all the important people — your parents, your children, your friends, your co-workers, your employer — and evaluate what's happening in your relationship with them. When it begins to deteriorate, put a time limit on the relationship — five-minute, one-hour, one-day persons. Maintain quality time!

To maintain your individuality, it is very important to avoid commingling of energies. (Figure 7) Allow the pure Life Energy to flow between you and your loved ones and not exchange the negative feelings and thoughts. *What you give your attention to or concentrate on becomes more.* If you really want to help your loved one, you will not allow him or her to sap your energy by reacting to the negative that he or she is experiencing. There is no limit to the Life Energy in you; so there is no need to draw It from someone else to feel good.

For example, a husband comes home from work and is feeling tired after a bad day, but he doesn't want to pass this feeling onto his family; so he comes to the door and puts on a happy face before he enters the house. He pretends, but the subconscious mind knows he is tired. The wife has had a high-energy day. She greets him at the door and sees his happy face and reacts to that, then suddenly she feels uncomfortable. Her subconscious mind picks up on the tiredness, and since high energy flows to low energy, she feels drained. As the evening goes on, he feels better and she feels miserable. Later, they go to bed and sleep in each other's energy fields. This is where he really drains her. The next morning, she can hardly get out of bed, and he goes off to work feeling terrific. During the day, she builds up her energy again, and that evening the cycle starts over.

Adjusting Your Aura

The way to end this negative cycle is by recognizing and calling upon the Power and Presence within you. It is limitless and inexhaustible. Make a statement,, "I now call upon the Divine Light within me to fill my space. I now seal off so that only good that belongs to me comes in and good goes out." It helps if you get a mental picture; so you can visualize this energy as a stream of golden energy that is beamed from your forehead, and you can fill your force field from top to bottom and from side to side — like stepping into an ovoid bubble of light.

To physically adjust your aura: Stand up and rub your hands together until you feel heat. Start above your head and begin brushing through your aura. This is like taking an invisible shower. Begin to work in your force field, concentrating on yourself. Take a deep breath and let go of all the negative energy. Rub your hands together again and run them around the body until you get goose bumps, until you feel an energy change, like changing gears in a car. Again, take a deep breath and enjoy the release. Seal off your space with the Light and affirm, "Only good goes in, and only good goes out."

Another way to physically clean up your energy field is to take a shower. Add to the shower mental imagery and see that water running through you and cleaning your whole energy system, taking all the negative vibrations down the drain. Visualize surrounding yourself with pure white light. Suddenly you will feel like you've had two nights' rest.

When you feel the negativity entering your space, you can affirm silently, "I do not accept this. I now fill my force field with white light, and I seal it off so only good comes in and only good goes out." You can clean up the space in your home using the same technique. Just as you clean it out physically, it can be done spiritually by affirming, "Only love, truth, and healing fill these rooms. The light surrounds my property, letting in only Good." The higher source of energy controls the lower source of energy; so use yourself as a source of healing energy and let it radiate out into the rooms of your home or office. Energy usually comes into the left hand and goes out from the right. (It's the opposite for left-handed people.) Identify with the Power within you and let the energy flow. By doing this, you create a loving, healing atmosphere, an atmosphere of oneness and creativity where people can relax and be themselves immediately.

Your Aura and Others

Once you start cleaning up your space and sealing off, your friends may notice a difference in you. You have changed, and you are not reacting to their energy as you once did. The connection or control they had over you is broken, and they feel uncomfortable about it. Friends who drained you may accuse you of not loving them anymore, and then try to induce guilt to get you to acquiesce. All you have to say is "I love you. I am just changing my behavior patterns, and the relationship is changing for the better!"

When you deal with others, think of them as energy. To keep a relationship growing and flowing, you energize each other. Using the former example, now when the husband comes through the door, he can greet her and say, "Honey, give me five minutes of your good energy." She knows he is there sapping her, and she knows how to replenish her energy by speaking her word or meditating. The husband gets the energy he needs and can sustain it, and they don't drain each other.

You can help people who are ill by using this technique. When people are ill, their energy field is down, it's negative. They need energy to lift their vibration to bring them up to the pattern of wholeness. The pattern of well being, of healing, is a certain vibration. When a person's energy vibration is down on any level and it is kept down, like a low level of electricity coming into an appliance, it will burn out. It won't work or function correctly. To raise people's energy levels, you can give them a hug. Wrap your arms around them and give them the energy. Then you fill back up with your own spiritual energy so you won't go away depleted.

When you know you are low in vibration, for example the emotional level, take a deep breath, surrender to the Presence and fill yourself with Light. ("Light" is another way or word expressing Spiritual Energy.) This way you are not tempted to go to someone else and take energy.

This sapping can also be done by voice. If you have a friend who calls and tells you about a headache and you talk about how horrible headaches are and how much they hurt, at the end of the conversation the caller will hang up and the headache will be gone, and you will have it. You identified with the problem (*the caller's* problem), and took it into your space.

This leads you to another technique. Work in the silence, and as someone is telling you about problems, you can say, "Oh, no." By doing this you are acknowledging the other person, and at the same time, you are saying "no" to the problem, so you are not identifying with it!

In Truth, if you unify with the Perfect Pattern within yourself and with the Perfect Pattern within the other person, in spite of their negativity, you will energize the pattern of wholeness in both of you. (The blessing technique.)

If someone is lying to you, bless the Truth in you and the Truth in the other person, and the lying cannot continue. Before they know it, they have told you the truth; or you know inwardly and are not deceived.

Learn to listen to your inner self and not go by outward appearances and statistics. This is more than just positive thinking. It is creative thinking.

There are many ways to be depleted. You function on five levels — physical, emotional, social, mental, and spiritual. A physical drain occurs when someone in need of energy puts his arms around you or just touches you. One example of this is ill elderly people with youngsters. Grandma, who doesn't feel well, wants to hold the child and be close. The child gets tired and cranky and eventually doesn't want to go see Granny anymore. It's because the child's getting depleted. The solution here is for the parents to seal the child off before they go to visit the grandma, or better yet, teach children to seal off. They can then enjoy Grandma and not be depleted. The mental and emotional drain happens when someone or something causes you to react. When you react, you also become a victim. Reverse this when Grandma is well and centered, and the child is not feeling well — the child will borrow energy from her and feel better.

Anyone, anywhere can trigger your emotions if you let them in. Teenagers are masters at draining parents emotionally. They get mom and dad so angry that finally they open up their space and let them in; thereby, giving the teens all their power. The parents become the victims. The teenagers feel great because they just had a successful power trip.

There is no time or space on the emotional, mental, and spiritual levels. If you think about a person a lot and feel drained or perhaps depressed, that person is probably depressed and thinking of you. You know you are happy and feeling good, but that other person is so depressed while thinking about you, your good energy is pulled from you, leaving you depressed!

You are a sending and receiving center of thoughts and emotions. There is a family vibration, a city vibration, a state vibration, a national vibration, and a person-to-person vibration. All vibrations from all thought are going around the planet. If you're not in control of your own space and everybody's down, then you'll be down, too. When there is tension in your country or your leader is under attack, a wave of depression can cross the country. If your aura was open, you would be affected by the surge of fear and uncertainty. By staying centered, you are not affected.

Everything is an outpicturing of the energy that you're using. The people in Washington, D.C. are an outpicturing of our thoughts at a national level. As a common national thought, we indicate that all politicians are rotten. What that thought does is create that situation. Instead, if you desire good honest politicians, you can think in terms of attracting creative, honest people who are dedicated to freedom and national service.

When you stay in control of your aura and maintain it, the higher energy takes you through any negativity. Passing thoughts have power, just as constant thoughts do at the level of your acceptance. Choose! Stand guard at the doorway of your mind! Take charge of your aura!

On the mental level, if you are thinking in negative terms, your emotions and body will be affected. This is why when you become aware of your thoughts, you can begin to consciously change the negative with an affirmation, in the now, and maintain wholeness and balanced energy in your aura.

Chapter Seven

Dynamic Tools for Empowerment

All of the following tools are to direct your life from the inner consciousness. They are to guide you beyond the mind to the Source of your spiritual self and to direct the power to heal, to reveal the truth, to guide you into right action and appropriate answers to any situation. These tools shift your awareness to a center of peace, poise, and power so you can live your life at the highest level possible. Dramatic changes take place when you practice these methods as directed.

The Blessing Technique

To get your energy system under control, you can use the unifying or blessing technique. This is done by consciously identifying with the Perfection within you and the Perfection within another person. By doing this, every time you converse with someone you will bring the communication to its highest level. On the spiritual level, there is only one, there is only the truth of the situation, which is good for both parties on the spiritual level. There are no language barriers. There is only complete understanding, complete knowing, and complete love. There is no separation, there are no strangers! We are one family in the universe, as individualized expressions in physical form. We're all the same energy expressing it uniquely.

• The bless-and-blast technique. There are times when you are too emotionally charged to stay centered. You may be yelling and screaming, but when you use the blessing technique in the silence, you have the Spiritual Energy doing its perfect healing work, and then something constructive is experienced in the confrontation, and a clearing takes place to create a better understanding. You stay in charge of you and your space, and both people benefit in some way.

Silently bless the good in you and the good in another person, then express how you feel. You don't ever have to be phony. It is vital to be open and honest with others. Never repress or suppress emotional energy. Use an "I" message to say how you feel. Frustration only causes more frustration. But if you discharge the energy properly, you clean up the misunderstanding in communications and create a constructive atmosphere for growth.

As you center your being, you function more effectively and efficiently right where you are. There is no need to run and hide from negative people or situations. You can experience the good in all and in everything, diffusing the negative.

• Use the blessing technique to prepare your day (because anything you give your attention to increases in vibration), and it goes more smoothly, harmoniously. With this tenet, you can bless the good in yourself and the good in your home, your car, your appliances, your clothing, or anything, and you get a much better performance from them. It adds magnetism to everything you have blessed, and it uplifts you.

The blessing technique means you consciously say in words, "I now bless the good in me and the good in another person, place, or situation." You set up a powerful energy. On this level there is no resistance. Everything is one. The person and the place are energized without depleting you!

• You can test this with a housefly. You've had some heavy programming about houseflies. Namely, they're dirty and they carry diseases. A change of attitude is called for now. Another perception of the fly is that it is a magnificent little thing. It is divine order, it is energy in motion, it's little filmy wings support its chubby little, hairy body. It's a miracle in flight, and it encourages decay so the world is not filled with garbage. It has a purpose and a function in the universe, as you do. So why pick on a little fly and swat at its pesky, hairy body? The fly just doesn't belong in your space. How can you set up an exchange of communication with the housefly? All of life is constantly flowing through the same medium, the subconscious, and you can direct and control the fly through the subconscious. Relax, into the proper tension to use this energy effectively. It requires a calm state of mind. Unify with the perfect energy within you and the perfect energy within the fly. In your mind, call the fly to the back of your hand. "Fly, I unify with the Divine Intelligence within you, and I command you to come to the back of my hand." The fly will come and sit on your hand. (It's not fair to squash him when he does!) Hold it with your thought and take it outside. What you have done is claim your space. With love, you take care of something that doesn't belong in it.

This technique does something to your psyche. If you can do this with a fly, you can do it with ants at a picnic. You can use it out camping to keep snakes away. You can control your space wherever you are. If you use this energy with love or with the Higher Power, you send a beam of light energy before you and it clears the way so you are safe and secure in whatever you do. All of life is for you, not against you! This takes a lot of fear out of moving into new experiences.

• When you are truly involved with living from your Inner Self, sometimes things seem to get worse before they get better because you energize all the patterns in your subconscious, and they are pushed to the surface by inner growth. By adjusting your attitude about this process, you can say, "All that is happening right now is uncomfortable, but I am releasing worn-out conditions to make room for the better. I can see that the ego program in my subconscious was very negative, and I'm moving out the garbage. This too shall pass. My true life patterns evolve now! My life now has a dramatic change for the better!"

There will come a time when you live and move and have your being guided by Spirit on any level in perfect oneness, perfect peace, wholeness, prosperity, and joy, a time when words and thoughts are inadequate to describe what you are experiencing. Isn't it difficult to describe beauty? Is there a word to adequately describe a sunset or a flower? Enjoy this in silence and thanksgiving. Accept this infusion of healthy, good, whole energy — a sense of unity with everything and everyone. There are no boundaries, there is a sense of belonging and a connectedness with all of life. There is no loneliness when you come from the Spiritual Source, only Impersonal Love. It is limitless and eternal. It creates perfect harmony and understanding. You are inspired and uplifted!

Affirmations

Affirmations are basically used to help you stay in charge of your conscious mind, to direct the thought energy creatively. An affirmation is a positive statement made in the present tense. There is no time or space on the mental level, so now is all there is. There is only the ego belief in time. You are the only one who chooses to live in the past or the future. The words you use in an affirmation are important. It also directs the subconscious to act. The feedback from the subconscious or the image you get in mind must reflect your desired result. The words must cooperate with your desire. If you have a negative feedback to a word from the subconscious, change the word until you have a neutral response or until you have changed your belief system in your subconscious program. Affirmations work only when they are statements of what you know to be true. The most effective affirmations are ones of total acceptance and giving thanks of appreciation for it being done now, for example, "Divine Love is established in this situation now."

Other examples of useful affirmations are:
- "Divine order is established in all of my experiences now." This is effective when your world seems out of order and nothing seems to be coming together, or you are having financial difficulties.
- "I accept that divine timing is flowing in all of my affairs now." You can use this affirmation when your schedule seems scattered and everything is running late or you feel pushed to complete a task.
- "Spirit, mind, and body are working in perfect balance right now. Divine Energy is flowing through me, as me, in

proper tension for the task at hand." This is a good affirmation when you are tired, you are experiencing low energy, lack of vitality, and feeling out of sorts.

- "Divine harmony adjusts, heals, and harmonizes everything in this situation right now. This can be affirmed when you are out of harmony with people, places, and things.
- "Divine right action shows me the Way now for my greatest good." State this if you desire guidance or protection.
- "I now release and let go of that which does not belong to the truth of me, and I accept lovingly that which does belong to me for my highest Good." This is useful when you feel congested or that your pathway is blocked.
- "I am compelled by the Divine Presence within me to say the right thing, at the right time, and in the right way, to achieve my goal. This technique can be used when you are going on an interview or giving a presentation or answering a deposition and when you are not sure of what to say.

Meditation

Meditation is the way to the Power. It is a listening attitude. It is a way for you to tune in and turn on the Power, a way for you to get in touch with your Spiritual Being.

Transcendental Meditation

Why transcendental meditation and not other forms? To reach the Source, you must move beyond the five senses. The five senses monitor what's around you in the physical universe (the result of your present state of consciousness). The journey of true meditation moves past the mind, emotions, and body to the source of your being, to the superconscious — beyond thought to awareness. Many meditations are mentally involved in repeating affirmations or in listening to special music or visualizing certain images. These are helpful because they can calm and relax the body, but they really keep you locked into the instrument or personality (mind, emotions, and body), and you do not move beyond the personality.

The goal of transcendental meditation is to move beyond the five senses to the Creative Source or your sixth sense, intuition, and your true identity, which is your individuality!

Mechanics of Transcendental Meditation

Set aside two twenty-minute periods a day, with a minimum of four hours in between each meditation. Wait at least 45 minutes after you have eaten so the basic metabolizing of food will not be interrupted.

Set an alarm with a soft tone for the twenty-minute time period, and use this until the timing becomes automatic. Sit in a comfortable chair with both feet resting on the floor. (The reason for sitting is the body tends to go to sleep when in a reclining position.) Your back should be fairly straight.

Breathing is a very important part of the meditation. Begin breathing in through the nostrils, filling the lungs and slowly releasing through the mouth; then repeat. This helps calm the body and focus attention on the breath of life. You will notice that your breathing does slow down and all your systems go into a rest mode. This is normal; do not panic.

Take two or three minutes to become aware of the conscious mind and the distractions that might be present — an airplane flying overhead, a car motor, etc. Remember you are on a journey. You are moving your focus from the outer world to the inner world. Observe your thoughts … let them come and go … be aware of the speed of your thoughts. There is no resistance to anything in meditation … just a flowing past any distraction with the aid of a mantra.

What is a Mantra?

A mantra is a sound, not a word. This is important because if you use a word that has meaning to you, you get caught on the mental level. And remember, the goal is to move past the mechanism, the instrument of mind, emotions and body to the Superconscious. A mantra is a sound that you repeat over and over again to keep your spiritual focus. It is a sound that has the frequency of the Universal Truth, God or Life Force. When the mantra is done sufficiently, it gets into a certain kind of vibration that is in harmony with the universe — into a certain state of consciousness.

When you feel you are ready, start saying the mantra, *Satnam*, and keep repeating it over and over for the remaining time. Let the speed of your thoughts determine the speed of your mantra. When your thoughts slow down, let the mantra slow down. When your thoughts speed up, speed up the mantra. There is no such thing as a bad meditation when using the mantra for coming into the Presence; there is only an active or a passive meditation. After the soft bell alarm has sounded, take about two or three minutes to come out of meditation. This allows your breathing, your heart rate, all your systems to return to normal from a deep state of relaxation.

When you're in a meditative state, you are connecting with that Perfect Pattern and Power, that Spiritual Presence within that is all-knowing, all-wise, everywhere-present — all Love, Peace, and Poise, all the healing Power.

In meditation, you do not hear voices. If you do, you are caught up in the psychic energy (the ego, the past and future). Your mantra is a protection that carries you through any bombardment of things that don't belong in your space during meditation. Meditation refines your energy and moves you into areas of more beauty, oneness, and nowness.

Work towards doing it twice a day. If your lifestyle doesn't permit this schedule, you don't have to feel guilty for missing a meditation. There's a right time for everything, however, keep in mind the tremendous benefits you receive.

Our Western culture often believes that if a little bit is good, a lot is much better. If one aspirin is good, ten will create a miracle! Sometimes you may think that meditation is so good that you want to stay there. Spirit, mind, and body must work together on this planet earth, and staying in a trance floating off somewhere, makes you "so heavenly inclined that you are no earthly good." You have work to do here. You meditate, connect, clear the way while meditating, and then you act.

On the other hand, if you are deeply troubled, two or three days in meditation will help you. You need spirit, mind, and body working together to heal. Take this time so the mind can quiet down, and when the mind is in balance, Spirit will lead the emotions and the body into balance. Then you move into right action and right experience.

Meditation is of tremendous benefit to the body. It slows down the circulation and the metabolism so the body can go into deep rest which gives the body a chance to rejuvenate and revitalize.

In meditation, you're moving towards the silence, and your ego mind will rebel. It may say to you, "Twenty minutes! You've got better things to do than that!" The ego must give up control, and it doesn't do that easily. Your mantra takes you past the ego to your true Self. Be patient, not perfect!

As you shift into an altered state of consciousness, you experience a calming energy. Thoughts may come into your conscious mind. Let them come up because if you release thoughts in meditation, you don't have to experience them in your outer life experiences. Thoughts occurring during your meditation are not ruining it. You're releasing and letting go of thoughts that are creating tension in your system, whether they are labeled good or bad. Over stimulation of the positive is just as harmful as depletion by the negative. Balance is the ideal. Let the thoughts come and go, and don't fight them or follow them. Just keep the mantra going. Adjust the repetition of the mantra to the speed of the thoughts. Stay focused on the mantra.

With your feet on the floor, you are grounding any overabundance of energy that your body is not refined enough to handle. Part of the process is fine tuning your instrument so you can accept more power. You can place your hands flat on your lap with your palms facing upward, or if you are particularly low in vitality, place your hands on your lap with your index fingers touching your thumbs to keep the energy in your own system. Since the energy flows in the left and out the right side, generally your left hand goes under the right hand.

You are shifting into an altered state of consciousness, a lower frequency, a listening attitude, an alert awareness, and a state of rest. Don't panic at the difference in your energy level, just keep your mantra going at your own pace.

At times when you are feeling ill, just lie down, using pillows to support your body's stress points — under the neck, knees, and arms, and repeat your mantra. It will lift you and bring you into a higher energy for healing. Different things can happen during a meditation, for example, you may start crying. Cry and keep your mantra going. If something interrupts you, keep the mantra going. Eventually you will gain control over what's trying to distract you from your meditation.

Generally, meditating energizes you, so it is not to be done right before you go to bed. If you are highly stressed, you may fall asleep; so it can be done at bedtime. Pick the time that is right for you. The benefits are tremendous and amazing — more peace, experiencing oneness. It dissolves stress and places you in the perfect place at the right time in the right way. You have more clarity, and you are more effective, more efficient, more aware of your intuitive nature. Basically, it connects you with the teacher within you.

Spiritual Mind Treatment

Meditation is the way to the Power, and Spiritual Mind Treatment is the use of the Power.

In this world you have needs and desires. Just as you turned on the Power in meditation, you can direct it for a specific use through thought and words. Work on your list of needs and desires to define them specifically. The more specific you are in mind and detailed about the desire itself, the quicker you will manifest it in form. The faster the formless takes form, the faster the invisible becomes visible. Thoughts becomes things. Do not concern yourself with how this is to be done; it's still a mystery. It just works!

The technique of directing the Higher Power for a specific demonstration is called Spiritual Mind Treatment. You train your mind to accept and identify with your spiritual identity, the perfection within you. In Spiritual Mind Treatment, you speak your word in the present for a specific use of this Power. You are initiating a specific action to get a specific result.

Spiritual Mind Treatment is used when you are relaxed because the way you do something is the way something manifests. If you put your desire in word form and in a certain structure while you're upset or angry, then that's the way you will demonstrate your desire. For everything to come into your life lovingly, gently, harmoniously, you must be in the best frame of mind possible when you work with this particular tool.

Spiritual Mind Treatment (Figure 8) uses five steps: recognition, unification, realization (speaking your word), thanksgiving, and release. The use of these fives steps aligns your mind with the Universal Creative Intelligence. Stay in the now, and speak your word affirmatively in the present tense to initiate this law of love or law of energy into action. Spiritual Mind Treatment is not holding thought because thoughts that are held are going nowhere, and everything in the universe is energy in motion. You give this energy a form or a shell to fill with your words and thoughts.

In a Spiritual Mind Treatment you can treat for anything — a car, a house, money, wardrobe — any material thing. Go beyond that. Treat for emotional balance and health, for mental well being, for right ideas, for inspiration, and you'll keep progressing to where your material needs are met. Right ideas come to help you succeed and develop that Inner Self that you are meant to be. Then you will move into the inspired life where your life is flowing and you are in tune and centered most of the time, and whatever you do, you prosper and so does all of mankind.

As you move into this state of grace, your words and thoughts almost instantly manifest what you desire. You think about a certain person, and he or she calls you on the telephone. You desire certain information and you pick up a book or the newspaper, and there it is. It always comes through people, places, and things. The information you need is always at your fingertips, and you don't need to go through volumes of books to find it.

– Figure 8 –

SPIRITUAL MIND TREATMENT

Spiritual mind treatment is the use of the Power.
It is the personalization of the impersonal power.

The five steps involved in spiritual mind treatment are:

1. **Recognition.**

2. **Unification.**

3. **Realization or speaking your word.**

4. **Thanksgiving.**

5. **Release.**

– Figure 9 –

SPIRITUAL MIND TREATMENT

The Law of Mind is set into motion with words and thoughts. Words and thoughts give form to the formless divine energy. Actually every word that is spoken is a treatment, to the degree of belief and feeling that is expressed. Words give direction and focus to the Law of Mind, and feelings give it intensity or the dynamic energy.

The Five Steps in the Method of Spiritual Mind Treatment

1. **Recognition** — Recognize that there is a Power and Presence within you that is greater than you are. This Life Energy, operating as Intelligence, permeates all things, places and people. It is the Source of Life. It is the integrity of the universe, always operating as Divine Order, Divine Balance, Divine Timing or Rhythm, and Divine Harmony. It is the Perfect Power and Pattern. It is limitless, everywhere present, all powerful and eternal. It is Oneness. all the Love there is… It is the One Creation and Creator.

2. **Unification** — You are what this Power is. Now affirm that your mind is an individualized expression of the Divine Mind. You are love, peace, harmony and all good right where you are. This Divine Substance expresses through every part of your being, as you. You have all the attributes of this Divine Intelligence now. You are what It is, and It is what you are.

3. **Realization (speaking your word)** — The word "realization" is "to make real." In this step, you willingly give up false beliefs, opinions and attitudes. This is the point at which you create the mold of thought. You state your affirmations in the first person and in the present tense. This is a clear acceptance by the mind that the thought you are thinking can and does become demonstrated in your life. You declare your word to be the presence, power and activity of Divine Spirit and speak it with authority because the Law, directed in Love, is a servant of Spirit.

   Examples: "I now accept the perfect healing presence within me." "I am a reflection of the prosperity of the nature of good around me and make greater use of my talents and abilities." "I am led and guided to make right decisions and to take right action."

   Visualization is of great value during this step. Paint a mental picture, with you in it. Anticipate, expect the result desired. Feel that your words are more than just words. They are objects and ideas becoming manifest in your life now!

4. **Thanksgiving** — You express gratitude that your treatment is a new mental cause set in motion and that it is manifesting right now. The demonstration is accomplished in Divine Mind. You give thanks for the good that is already yours. "Before they call, I will answer."

5. **Release** — You mentally let go and let the Law of Mind do the work. Act as if the demonstration has already occurred. Affirm and reaffirm its completeness. Accept it as being so right now. Know that you have set the Law in motion. And it is done!

– Figure 10 –

Spiritual Mind Treatment

Instructions: Put this on a tape recorder.
Use your voice and play it back one or more times daily.

For Betterment of Conditions

There is one Life. That Life is perfect. That Life is the Divine Intelligence expressing in and through all things. There is one Mind. That Mind is perfect, and that Mind is my Mind now. I am what It is and It is what I am.

I now speak my word and accept easily, lovingly, and gently.

Everything that I do or think is governed by Divine Intelligence and inspired by Divine Wisdom. I am guided into right action. I am surrounded with friendship, love and beauty. Enthusiastic joy, vitality and inspiration are in everything I do.

I now release all worn out conditions and completed situations to their True Life Place, and they release me to my True Life Place. In the Power and Presence, I live, move, and have my being. A complete sense of happiness, peace and certainty floods me with Light. I have confidence in myself because I am Divine Presence. The Divine Presence within me is all-wise, all-knowing, everywhere present and all-powerful.

The Spirit within me reveals the answer to any condition, situation, or challenge which confronts me. I know that the answer is revealed here and now. It is within my own mind because the Divine Presence is right where I am. I accept the answer in calm confidence, in perfect trust, in abiding faith and with complete peace. I accept my good now.

I know exactly what to do in every situation. Every idea necessary to successful living is brought to my attention. The doorway to ever-increasing opportunities for self-expression is open before me. I am continuously meeting new and greater experiences. Every day brings some greater good. Every day brings more blessings and greater self-expression. I am prospered in everything I do.

I open myself to prosperity. I give thanks for my unexpected good now. I joyfully accept my divine inheritance. I know that what is mine will claim me, know me, rush to me. The presence of Spirit is me. The mind of Spirit is my mind. The freedom of Spirit is my freedom. Everything I do prospers me in every way.

Today I bestow the essence of Love upon everything. My soul meets the soul of the universe in everyone. This Love is a healing power, turning everything into wholeness. I am now expressing the rhythm of life. I give thanks for perfect health now. I am at home in the Divine Presence wherever I am.

I am grateful. And so it is.

Spiritual Mind Treatment helps you get to the state where you can key into that Self where there is no time, no past, and no future — it's all wisdom and knowledge. This power will fluctuate as you go through levels of growth. At times everything you desire manifests, then you will hit a certain plateau. At this point, you go through releasing more worn-out conditions or completed situations. As you release more debris from the subconscious, your world seems to become worse before it becomes better. This is revealing to you what the subconscious needs to release, the old patterns that are blocking your demonstration. During these times, use the Spiritual Mind Treatment technique to achieve calmness, to achieve right action, to achieve whatever your material needs are. Keep on keeping on with affirmations, blessing techniques, meditation, and treatment.

The law of mind is set into motion with words and thoughts. Words and thoughts give form to the invisible energy. (Figure 9) Actually every word that is spoken is a treatment, to the degree of belief and feeling that is expressed. Words give direction and focus to the law of mind, and feeling gives it intensity and the dynamic energy.

You can treat for anything — spiritual, mental, emotional, physical or social. If it's a relationship with someone you desire, speak your word "to be" something (to be happily married rather than to have a husband or wife). This means that if what or whom you desire is not for your highest and greatest good, its equivalent is there for you that is for your highest good.

Never treat to take something away from someone. If you do, that action will come back to you. If you get something by force, manipulation, or scheming, that is what you have to do to keep it — by using force, manipulation, scheming. When you deny someone their good, that good is denied to you!

By writing your treatments down, you can appreciate the results more accurately. If something is left out of the treatment, it's not the Law's fault. Instead of blaming the Law and thinking it doesn't work for you, you can look at your treatment and see what you left out. An example of this is a woman in Los Angeles who wanted a book store. She didn't have a lot of money, but she knew books, and she liked to work with people. She treated for the right location for the book store and for lots of people coming into it. That is what manifested. The store was in an ideal location, lots of people came, but business was not good. She forgot to treat for people to buy the books! So she went back and corrected the treatment, and the bookstore is now flourishing.

It's very important not to outline how the answer is accomplished in your treatment. A statement like, "I need an increase in pay to do this," is a limitation. You keep creating the need. Be specific in *what* you desire, but don't get into the *how* of the way it manifests. It is not known how it works — it is only known that it works!

Visualization can be used in Step Three. The picture you have helps you to get a stronger idea of what you desire. For example, a woman desired a car. She treated for a gold Dodge Caravan. She went to a dealership and rode in the van to be able to mentally embody the idea and to get a feeling of it to empower the thought. She got a picture of it and put it on the refrigerator so she could see it every day, identify with it, and give thanks for it. The van in the picture happened to be blue. She really wanted a gold one, but she demonstrated a blue one because that's what she had been visualizing. Every time she looked at her refrigerator, she sent a photo message of a blue van to her subconscious mind. And that's what was demonstrated. When the blue one came, she could have turned it down. She decided she preferred it. She could have said no to the blue one while affirming, "I know my treatment is manifesting, but this isn't the right car," and then waited for the gold one. An important point to be made is that you are in the picture, that is, see yourself driving the van. Make your visualization as close to reality as possible.

Don't limit yourself with just visualization. Sometimes your consciousness has the ability to achieve a demonstration that is better than you realize. That's why you state, " ... or its equivalent." Consciously you may desire one image, but subconsciously you may be accepting another image. And it's the subconscious acceptance that produces the demonstration.

It is very important to have only one person treating for you on a specific thing or have a group who is supporting one treatment. Asking everyone you meet to treat for you creates many different answers and causes confusion. It also suggests superstition and doubt.

It is wise to start with the five steps of Spiritual Mind Treatment until you fully understand the method and until you are demonstrating enough so you can trust the words you speak. Continue to treat for your desires. Put your treatments on 4" x 6" cards, and every morning after you meditate, just quickly go over the cards and accept. If you get a strong doubt about your treatment, repeat it. If you don't, release it, knowing it is coming into your life at the right time, and at a time that you can sustain it. Follow up with a Spiritual Mind Treatment for acceptance.

Treatments always work at the level of your acceptance. If your treatments are not working for you, there are a few things you can ask yourself. Thoughts of criticism and condemnation block a treatment. If you're criticizing anyone, you're holding back your good. Criticism blocks Spirit, so become accustomed to the idea of finding good in every situation, not negative condemnation.

When you did your treatment, did you relax? If you didn't relax, you haven't let go. You must relax into peace or the Spiritual Mind Treatment is blocked by tension. Possessing people, places, and things will also stop the flow. There is a natural law of circulation in the universe — what goes out comes back multiplied. Don't hold back and think there's not enough to go around. The universe has a limitless supply; it is an abundant universe. Any denial of another person's good is a denial of your own good.

These are points to check if you are not demonstrating:
- Have you created a vacuum in consciousness, released the old to make room for the new?
- Have your forgiven yourself and others?
- Is your treatment in the now, in the present tense?
- Have you released your treatment to the Law and gone on about the task at hand?

- Thoughts of criticism and condemnation block your treatments.

The things that are right for you signal when you are on the right path. You move in order, right timing, harmony, and balance, and you flow in the now. Then you know that you are in some facet that is important to the end result of your True Life work. Some people are led in many directions — a little accounting here, a little public relations there, a little acting or public speaking, and they end up being a great master teacher.

When you use Spiritual Mind Treatment to achieve your goal, treat then let go. Get on with the task at hand as you work easily, lovingly, and gently toward your goal. Don't just sit and expect God to do the work. God's work is done. Nothing is incomplete in the universe. The pattern of completion is right where you are, and it's within you. Since you are a part of the Greater Process or God in action, you have the answer within you. You are to be true to your Spiritual Mind Treatment in mind and in action. Be single-minded, decisive, trusting, silent, and steady in the unfoldment of the answer.

Treat and do what you know to do. The moment that you are blocked on the pathway, you stop and check out any confusion, doubts, fears. Get centered, and the answer is there! Don't move in confusion. Get centered. Wait for clarity.

Five-Minute Imagery Exercise

Relax. Sit down for five minutes and visualize yourself in the completed project. Start with getting the right idea. Once you get it and you accept the right idea, then you treat for the means by which to support this idea. Then things start happening at the level of your acceptance.

The end result may not happen the way you think it should. That's getting into the "how" again. Stay out of the how. You can work out a lot of the ego feedback about "how" in a five-minute imagery exercise, or you may get a complete picture and decide that isn't what you want at all. This exercise helps you to be more specific in your treatment by helping you work out some ideas that you think are good, but may not be what you want at all.

In the five-minute imagery exercise, you can go over advantages and disadvantage of one or the other. Using a note pad and pencil is useful. Note down the feedback, then review the lists and decide.

At night, go to your subconscious mind and say, "Okay, subconscious mind, reveal to me what I need to know to make this decision." You may awaken in the middle of the night. Keep your pencil and paper handy so you can write your thoughts down. Put your feet on the floor and come fully awake and write your thoughts down. You might wake up in the morning flooded with ideas — write them down whether or not they make sense. Do this for about a week, then tally up. There will be a pattern on the paper, and there's your answer.

The answers are within you. You simply need to practice a few skills to get them flowing.

Spiritual Mind Treatment is fascinating, and it works. The more you use treatment, the more effective you get. The Law is exact and precise. Every treatment is effective, but it won't come into your physical realm until you have accepted it, consciously and subconsciously. In treatment, you are consciously treating your mind to a completed idea. You keep working until you have consciously accepted it, and you've given a strong message to the subconscious mind. The moment you break through the doubt barrier, the subconscious has to produce. That is its function. When the conscious and the subconscious minds agree, you demonstrate. It will be where you can touch it and experience it.

Chapter Eight

Emotional Control

To demonstrate anything, you have to demonstrate emotional balance. To get the mind centered at all, you have to get out-of-control emotions under control. The emotions follow where the mind goes and what you concentrate on experiencing.

The ideal for our participation in the Universal Divine Intelligence is for life energy to flow freely through you as you. Thoughts are to flow easily through your mind, and feelings are to flow freely through your body. When this is not happening, you develop blocks and discomfort in your experiences. Always remain the witness or observer of your mind, emotions, and body so you can make changes when this flow is impeded.

Judging and labeling a feeling or adding a thought to the feeling creates a reaction, and then there is an emotional response. Emotions are reactions to outer input and are expressing the ego self, the outer programmed self. Whereas, feelings come from Spirit, the Divine Intelligence within. Feelings are not necessarily to be understood. They just are! Blocks are only developed when they are judged.

Emotional control is studied by examining the difference between emotions and feelings. Emotions are destructive. (Figure 11) They are fundamental qualities of your personality that create victims. The constructive feelings are love, faith, patience, trust, and come from the Divine Intelligence within. Destructive emotions are fear and all its attributes — hate, resentment, hostility, anxiety, anger, tension, guilt, reward and punishment, rejection, betrayal and abandonment.

– Figure 11 –

EMOTIONAL CONTROL

Feelings (Constructive)

Love — felt as a dynamic state of consciousness, rather than an emotion. Joy. Givingness, forgivingness, sincerity, graciousness, generosity, honesty It is not a desire to be loved or to love, but just Being. Never associate behavior with love.

Faith — Real faith is the conviction that the creative law is active in every thought of the mind. It moves you from "I believe" to "I know."

Patience — Everything comes under the law of growth, flowing in divine timing, not ego timing.

Integrity — Working from the inside out. It is natural and intuitive. Reverence for the spiritual in all of life. Honor comes from your integrity.

Trust — Trusting the spiritual energy at the heart of everything, and not putting your trust in another person. Divine wisdom reveals the truth in every situation. Trust It, rather than the ego self of people or appearances or facts. Trust Life, not people's behavior.

Compliments phrased with an "I" message are opinions — "I think you look great." They come from your own space and you are responsible for them.

Transformation — the way of attention. Do one thing at a time. Focus, and give full attention to the task at hand (an attitude of oneness). Always pay attention to the now.

Emotions (Destructive)

Hate — Jealousy, anger, envy, revenge, resentment, hostility, betrayal, rejection, greed, self-condemnation, criticism, judgement, depression.

Fear — of abandonment, loneliness, anxiety, tension, frustration.

Impatience — Force, manipulation, coercion.

Loyalty — This is seeking approval. Respect, approval seeking, a judgement.

Guilt — Dealing with comparison, competition, past and future. Living up to someone else's values. The cure is to stay in the now.

Possessiveness — of persons, places and things. That which belongs stays with you; there is no need to hold onto your good too tightly.

Compliments with "you" messages — "You look great" can make a person defensive because it's getting into their space and judging.

Denial — a way of avoidance.

Reward and punishment — when you are living fully in the now, you are not interested in praise or criticism.

Pre-thinking and preprogramming — Assuming thoughts for another person, e.g., "If I say this, she is going to think…" It's getting into another's space. You are unique, and each sees the world a little differently.

Divine Love is the most powerful force in the universe. It is the basic fundamental power of your individuality, your spirituality. It is pure awareness, beyond knowledge. It is pure feelings. It functions as Oneness. You came into this world with all the love you'll ever have. It's within you because you are a totally self-contained unit. You can't really give love. It is something that you must experience, and you give out the results of love you are feeling. The degree to which you love and accept yourself is the degree to which you can love another person. Everyone outside of you is an outpicturing of you; so the way you feel about people mirrors your feelings in form.

When you don't like someone, you're really saying you don't like yourself. When you bring love to the situation and identify with Power and Presence within you, you create an aura of harmony where healing can take place. Since you have all the love within you that you can ever experience at the level of your acceptance, you don't have to go outside yourself and think a person, place, or thing is going to bring love to you. They may trigger the vibration within you, but it won't sustain itself unless you totally accept it within yourself first.

When you desire a person, place, or thing, it can become a possession or a dependency or an obsession. This love is conditional. (See Figure 7) In this instance, you are really saying, "I love you as long as you fulfill my expectations. I love you as long as you're seeking my approval." That is not love, that is bondage. When you love someone, you love them whether they are hateful or loving. You just love, even if you do not like the behavior. It is important to separate behaviors from people. You don't have to like a person's actions to love the person.

Love is like the ocean. It doesn't hold back. It will give you what you want, a bucket or a cupful. It will express through you at the level of your acceptance. When you take a cup of water from the ocean, it doesn't tell you that's all there is; instead, it just flows back in and fills the vacuum.

The Divine Love within you has depth beyond understanding. Love is the cohesive factor that holds the universe together. It is harmonious. It is ever available and limitless. Love in the universal system is impersonal and unconditional. When you can love without personalizing it, you give love its greatest power. The truest love is one without attachment, obstacles, expectations, or agendas. That's the goal for you to reach. Then you have freedom. You can love and let go without hurting.

If you are lonely, frustrated, or feeling that no one loves you and you can't get into a meaningful relationship, it's because of where you are in your understanding of love. Usually there is a price tag, agenda, or expectation of some kind on it. Develop love as a givingness and forgiveness.

Love is a result of a feeling within you. It is demonstrated from the inside of you to the outer world. Love can be expressed in many different ways — through touch, through forgiveness of yourself first then others, through verbalizing without fear.

Fear of rejection is one of the primary reasons you don't show love to others. You're afraid to tell someone you love them because you may get put down, or you're afraid to do something nice for someone because they may take exception to it, or you're afraid to hug someone because of what others may think. If you let rejection stop you, you may miss the greatest expression of love. An example of that is the relationship of a father who was a strong disciplinarian with his daughter. The father was harsh and unaffectionate. The daughter loved him, yet at the same time she was terrified of him. Many times in her youth, she wanted to crawl in his lap or hug him and tell him she loved him, but she didn't because she was afraid of rejection. Finally, as a young adult in her thirties when the daughter was leaving her hometown, she gathered courage and risked everything. She went up to him, put her arms around him, kissed him and told him goodbye and "I love you." The father paled and began to sob. Here was a person who desperately needed love, and his rejection was his own inability to express love. It had nothing to do with the daughter personally!

Move beyond rejection and fear, for those who reject you are in the most need of love. Don't take the rejection personally. It isn't your rejection, it is theirs. Be impersonal about it. If you feel rejection, let it pass, and love more!

It is important to work through your fears. I once worked with a very healthy forty-year-old woman who had five children. Because she did not develop her own identity, she developed fear. She became so fearful that she couldn't drive her car. She stayed in bed for two years. There was nothing physically wrong with her, but she lay in bed paralyzed with fear. Slowly, she began to work with these life giving tools. It took her some time, but she is now out and moving about, flowing with life. When you live your life fully and joyfully, you stop letting fear be the motivation and you live in Power and Love.

The true being who takes control and uses his or her Power is courageous, sets fear aside, and goes on to great experiences. Anytime you are feeling fear, you can choose — "Am I going to let that fear continue to control me, or am I going to choose the direction of my thoughts?" What you are thinking now is going to be more tomorrow because *more attracts more*, just as *like thoughts attract like things*. It's the magnetic law of attraction. *What you recognize, you give Power to*; so if you're recognizing fear, you're giving Power to it and you will experience more of it. Turn your mind to Spirit and surrender it to the healing power of Love. *You can't be two things at once and succeed.*

You can take charge and say to yourself, "It's a fact that I am experiencing fear, but it's not the truth in me. There is a Power and Presence within me that is greater than I am. It guides me, guards me, and protects me. This fear is not valid, and I do not accept it." Set aside the fear, and do it anyway. Keep working with the affirmations, the "I am" — "I am peace. I am Power right now." Work with the higher thought.

The higher use of energy controls the lower use of energy. As you use the higher thought, you will eventually move out of the fear.

Never shut down or hold back this Power. It is the healing power of the universe. It is the cohesive factor of your whole mechanism. It is the Power that holds everything in place in harmony. And It comes into your life in your own individual way when you move out of the ego and surrender to Spirit. When your love is expansive, you are free, and those who come into your experience are free. That takes a lot of maturity.

Love enough, and no one can hurt you. When you're hurt, it's because you have chosen to be hurt and you have personalized something that may have nothing to do with you. This indicates martyrdom. To love means being honest. Love is not loyalty; loyalty is living up to someone else's standards. You never need to seek approval. Love is integrity. It is being real. It is giving your very best as a way of life. Much of society is confused about what's right and what's wrong. Only you know in your heart what is right for you, and good is natural. So what you know and express in your own way is the right way for you. Love is within everyone. Wherever you are, if you have a need and turn to the love within you, someone will be attracted to you to help you. Life responds to Life! Life is for you, not against you.

There is always that hand to assist you. There is always life expressing through people, places, and things. There is love within you and around you, and it will come into your experience at the level of a law of attraction, at the level of your acceptance.

Love — Plant Experiment

An amazing experiment to prove the power of love can be done with plants. Put two seeds into separate pots in the same amount of soil. Water them equally. Put them side by side where you can talk to them. Talk to one plant in beautiful loving terms. Tell it how great it is, what a beautiful loving expression it is, and to keep on doing it's good work. Ignore the other one. The one you gave your positive attention to will grow twice as tall and twice as fast as the other one. If it works on a plant, imagine how it works on people.

When Someone Is Lying

Divine Love constantly reveals the truth. No one can lie in the presence of true impersonal love without it being revealed. They may try to lie to you, but in your subconscious, the truth will be revealed to you. If you need to know the truth in a situation, keep working with love. "I bless the Love within me. Divine Love reveals the truth within me and the truth in this situation. Divine Love heals. Divine Love harmonizes. Divine Love adjusts everything in this situation now."

Why do some people lie? It's because their love expresses fearfully. Their capacity to love is seeking approval, and when they lie to you, it's because they're afraid you won't love them anymore or approve of their behavior. They are afraid of rejection. And quite often that is exactly what happens unless you can see through the lie and help them to tell their truth.

Hate, Love, Faith

Hate is the absence of love. Hate is resentment and hostility. It is the way you have been trained to express in certain situations. You didn't come into this world hating or being hostile. These qualities are the result of programmed conditioning and are expressed by choice.

What about love and hate? Hate is a programmed emotion from the outer knowledge, the ego, and love is a natural feeling from the Divine Presence within. Love is the cohesive glue holding the universe together. Love is a natural experience, and since you are totally self-contained and came into this world with all the love you'll ever have, you know it is within you right where you are. You may say, "It's a fact that I'm experiencing hate right now, but I'm not giving power to it. I am Love. All the Love of the universe is right where I am now!" By saying that, you are directing your mind to change your emotion of hate to a feeling of love.

When you experience hate, you are only hurting yourself because it is your choice. When you hate another person, you are putting a law upon yourself because words and thoughts are reflected back to you, as from a mirror. If someone else wants to be negative and hateful, let them. Let it be their problem, don't make it yours. When you detach yourself and say silently to yourself, "I am love right now," you change the flow of energy. Soon you will feel the return of poise and a sense of well being. You experience an inner warmth of love, and you begin to radiate that energy. Other persons either have to become loving to stay in your presence or move away and take their hate away with them.

Do you find yourself resenting the alarm in the morning, waiting in line at the market, answering the doorbell, doing silly monotonous tasks? Are you cranky with service people? All you are succeeding in doing is creating more of the same unless you change your attitude and bring the loving, healing Power to the situation. Choose love. Direct your mind — it leads the emotions!

Faith is what the use of the Law is all about. It's not a blind faith. With faith, you move beyond "I believe" to "I know that I know". When you've demonstrated this enough, you begin to know that Law works; it exists. It is important to keep your conscious mind clear and focused on your truth, and the subconscious mind responds accordingly. The more specific you are in thought, the quicker the subconscious manifests the outer experience.

Because you don't demonstrate in every area doesn't mean that you don't know about the Law. When challenges do arise, don't get upset with yourself or the Law. Say, "Thank you, Life, I've got something to work on out here, and I'll get busy and make the changes necessary to succeed. The truth is revealed to me!"

Do one thing at a time, focus, and give attention to the task at hand (an attitude of oneness). It frees up your consciousness so changes can occur. Maybe you've treated for something and it hasn't happened. Perhaps you haven't gotten out of the way of the divine circuits to let your treatment demonstrate. Maybe you have not released the treatment to the Law by thinking about it all the time (analyzing, questioning, doubting). Create a vacuum. Release old and worn-out conditions. If you get your bloated nothingness out of the way of your treatment and be quiet and still long enough, your good will catch up to you. What you give to the Law demonstrates. Each time you have a demonstration, it deepens your faith.

Fear is a denial of faith. Since the law of attraction is at work, what you fear will come upon you. Separate from your fears. Many of them are way out of proportion for what is happening. Take charge from the mental level. Decide to do it anyway! It's your panic that creates your chaos.

Your security is in the understanding of the Universal Mind. People leave us, places can burn down and you can lose friends, and situations change. Life changes and people and things move out of your life. When you have completed a relationship or finished with a situation, let it go. Sometimes you clutter your life with worn-out conditions and completed situations by holding on too tightly.

Relationships can complete. There are many people today whose marriages are a lie. They're married strictly because of financial convenience or insecurity or low self-esteem. It's difficult building an intimate relationship because people are unique individuals by nature, and programming on marriage and love has been that the woman is to be under control of the man. The man is to be the aggressive partner who goes out and makes a living while the woman stays in the nest and raises the children. When a relationship reaches the point where the expectations of the partners restrict or inhibit each individual's full expression of the other's life, one personality submerges the other (Figure 7).

No personality can survive being submerged. There are two half-people trying to make a whole. It doesn't work! Two individuals must learn to harmonize and grow as individuals — that is a healthy relationship. Self-reliance is part of self-actualization, you can be amply rewarded for services rendered. Find your life work and be financially independent. You were born to prosper. Contribute in any way you can to building a relationship in which both people involved can grow and evolve to be free to live in harmony.

This is love at its highest, finest, and best. Yet, love is firm. It can say "no" in the right places! If you look at love as a development in growth within yourself, you can give more and more and more. The fountain doesn't cease, and it really is what makes the world go round.

Patience is the law of growth. When you treat for something, you don't want to force a demonstration. Operate in the law of growth or patience, and let your demonstration come in divine timing. You must let everything come into your experience at the right time so you can sustain it. When you start doubting that you are demonstrating, look at what is going on in your life and what is taking your mind off your goals. The more tense you get about it, the more you push it away from yourself. Do your affirmation and meditation and then release your goal. Focus on the task at hand.

While you're concentrating on the task at hand, staying in the now, you're not negating and blocking the demonstration, and it will move into your life in perfect order and perfect timing. If you force something into your life prematurely, you have to deal with keeping it in the same way. Often, good thoughts and good things are lost because they come into your life at the wrong time.

Guilt

Guilt comes from referring to past incidents. Do you compare yourself to the past programming and put yourself down because you may not be measuring up to someone else's standards? Perhaps old negative programming is referring to a certain type of behavior that is required in a certain situation, i.e., the perfect mother, the perfect student, the perfect teacher, the perfect father, the perfect professional person. You are already perfect on the spiritual level, the Real You. All that is required of you is to do your best. That is enough! You are enough for any situation.

What is past is past, and you're to let it go. If you bring guilt into the picture every day, you color your life with grey and gloom and doom. You paid the price for whatever you did when you did it; so you don't need to carry guilt around your neck like a millstone. If you look at the ultimate in the Law of Love or Life, the act was paid for at that time. When you make a mistake, you suffer the consequences. Subconsciously, if you're still carrying around with you the guilt of not measuring up to other people's images, work on these images, thoughts, and emotions and release them to their true life place. Let them go. There is no approval to seek! Be yourself! The world needs you, your talents, your love that expresses through you as you.

Forgiveness

To forgive is to cease feeling resentment towards an offender. Forgiveness is not denial, nor is it pretending to forgive and to forget. You need to make good decisions about forgiving. It is more than just an emotional response. You need to think about what you can forgive and forget, and what is still a problem. Just because you forgive someone does not mean you let the person keep on hurting you.

Forgiving means you stop making the other person responsible for your experience. You take responsibility for your choices and healing. First of all, work on forgiveness of yourself. In doing this, you understand what to forgive and when it's the right time to do that. You know when to stop carrying the load of the experience. You realize how unforgiveness stops your good and blocks the flow of Spirit in your life. You are not responsible for the other person's behavior. Separate the person from the behavior — "I love the Real You, but I don't like your behavior in this situation."

Everyday forgive yourself and forgive others (Figure 12). If you're feeling hostility towards someone, forgive them and release them. Get back into your own space and get out of theirs. Clean up your space with meditation and spiritual mind treatment until that someone no longer has any effect on you at all, and you are centered and neutral to the situation.

Here is an exercise to use when you are working with a person for whom you feel negativity. Get relaxed and, in your mind, place the person in a chair opposite you, and talk to them for five minutes or more in your imagination, rather than physically going to the person and attacking him or her. Unleash all your feelings, whatever they are. Talk out loud if you want to. Then, give the other person equal time. It's amazing how that person will talk back to you and give you new insights to the situation. It is all done in your imagination, and it's very powerful. Remember, we all use the same subconscious. Take responsibility for creating it all within your own consciousness. Let go and release,

– Figure 12 –

FORGIVENESS

Forgiveness simply means to give pardon without asking punishment.
Forgiveness dissolves whatever stands between you and your good.
It opens the way for your dreams to come true.

List any person, place, or thing that you are ready to forgive now.

1. **Resentments:**

2. **Anger:**

3. **Hostilities:**

4. **Jealousies:**

5. **Hate:**

6. **Denial:**

7. **Other:**

and the whole relationship is moved into a new place in your life. After a while, that person will disappear. If someone else appears in the chair, work with them in the same manner until guilt, resentment, and hostility of any kind are gone. When it is gone, you have neutralized the situation, and you have forgiven.

Reward and Punishment

Reward and punishment are actions you've been trained and conditioned to do from the time you were born. Starting with childhood, you are rewarded for being good. If you're good, you get a cookie. Later, in school you get rewarded if you get high grades or if you read well, and you're put down or punished if you don't.

With this kind of conditioning, you begin to think that if there's no one there to tell you that you're good, you're not good. As you graduate from your school group into your own lifestyle, the usual friends or teachers aren't there to say, "You did a good job today. You're a nice person. You're okay." Without this input, you begin to feel you are not okay; so you must be bad. This is an old value system. It doesn't work.

You were always good. You cannot destroy that. That is your divine inheritance. No matter what you do — how far down you go into the gutter or how high you go — you cannot destroy that Inner God Self. It waits upon you. That Good is always there. You can never deserve it. It is a gift from Life. You can't earn this gift. It is something that is given to you. You can't really earn your worth. You can only accept it.

Just accept yourself as you are and accept the day, the task at hand, in the now as it is. Get out of good or bad. They're only labels. Do your best. If it's not good for you, you'll be the first to suffer. You'll experience an unhappiness, a discomfort. You can change that by changing the thought behind it. Know that good is always within you to help you heal. The only punishment, then, is the punishment you place on yourself. Neither praise or criticism is important for your journey. Trust yourself and follow your inner Light. That is enough.

The Difference Between Emotions and Feelings

Whenever you succeed in stirring up feelings, you have made an impression that lingers. That person has responded with interest and attention, and you will be remembered. People do not remember you by any intellectual idea or concept you may have given them, but by how they felt in your presence.

Spirit, the Highest, all the Love you have, expresses through you in feeling. So if you keep your feelings free of the destructive emotions and reactive behavior, you will experience more of True Spirit, the flow of Life, unconditional love. The idea, the answer, the intuitive direction comes through as a feeling that you interpret through your mental atmosphere. To have any answers or any cooperation from Spirit, you must be relaxed physically into the proper tension and have emotional control. Stay centered!

Emotions are the result of judging feelings with a thought or an attitude attached. Emotions have more force and are more volatile than feelings. Emotions come from the five senses and your reaction to their input. Feelings are just feelings. They are natural and come from within, and they are to be allowed to flow freely as you observe them. Feelings express your intuition or your sixth sense, which comes from Spirit and is the language of Spirit.

To present anything in an effective way, you want to be persuasive, never aggressive or dominating. Forcing, manipulating, scheming, pushing, and being aggressive create more of the same, while being assertive is staking your claim and telling it like it is — from your own space, from a loving heart.

You work in and from your own space. Say what you think — "It's my opinion … I think … It seems to me … " And don't tell someone else how he or she should do something. This automatically makes another person defensive. You tell it like it is from your space, based on love and good intentions. If you want to use the art of confrontation with love, not resentment, first of all, elevate the situation to the spiritual level. If there is a person in your life who is disturbing you, mentally say in the silence, "I bless the good in me, and I bless the good in _____. I release you to your true life place and you release me to my true life place." That's love at its highest. True life place means wishing the other person the best. It doesn't mean the person will necessarily move out of your life but will move into your life in balance and in harmony. If someone is not meant to be in your life, they'll get out. Life will take them nicely away. You have taken control of your reactions, exercised your right to choose, and initiated the law to right action.

This is something you can use at work. When you have to work closely with people and you're constantly dealing with their good or bad moods, rather than firing people or forcing them to cooperate, go to work in the silence. Release them to their true life place. Life will take care of the change and create a vacuum. Then you draw into your experience people who work with you willingly and cooperatively.

Most of the work in this process is done in the silence. However, if you do have to confront someone verbally, get yourself centered in Spirit, and then use "I" messages. For example, if you're angry with someone and you've meditated and treated, but you still feel really steamed up and feel something must be said, use the blessing technique first, and then say, "I feel disappointment with your behavior" or "I'm displeased with this performance." Separate the behavior from the person. "This is what I feel about this type of behavior ... " These situations can cause tension with everyone in a relationship, and they need to be handled right away. When handled in an assertive manner with love, interesting things can happen. The other person may become your best friend or he may move out of your life peacefully. Don't wait until you are full of resentment. It is important to come from a center of love, and take care of it immediately.

The Laws of Attraction, Freedom, Balance

Emotional control operates under three basic laws — the law of freedom, the law of attraction, and the law of balance. The magnetic law of attraction draws situations and experiences to you at the level of your consciousness (what is around you is you). The way you get something is the way to keep that something. When you draw to you through Love or the mystical persuasiveness of Divine Spirit, it stabilizes that which comes into your life experience. It comes into your life by its own free will and it will stay in your life because you are free and it is free. No bonding or bondage — only Perfect Harmony. When you bond with someone, you are in each other's space — one of you is held back. When you harmonize as two unique individuals, each one has the freedom to expand his or her individuality.

Freedom is what life is all about. When you take another's freedom, you shut off the basic need of any natural being. The foundation of a living soul is to express freely. Love thrives in freedom. It is boundless, limitless and giving. Anything that is held in bondage or in any way loses its freedom, by its very nature will be looking for a chance to escape. Your self-integrity is violated when you possess another and deny them their freedom. It's like a ball and chain. When you release the thing that binds you, it also frees you!

When you release and let go of that which belongs in your life, it returns in a better way! By giving anything its freedom, you win it. That's the paradox. You never lose when you love enough. You can't. Isn't it the person who loves you the most that is the one who allows you to be your own self, whether you're nice or nasty or whatever? You are accepted for who you are — they love you, even if they don't like what you are doing. Usually that's parental love. Without any measure, it's just there. However, that means freedom through structure, honoring the natural laws of being (kindness, caring, generosity, harmony, order, and consideration). That's the law of attraction at work. You are drawn to a person like that — the friend who accepts you on your terms and you accept them in the same manner. You trust yourself in the relationship and exude love and support. There are no expectations or agendas.

Do not misunderstand the law of freedom. It is not a license to be irresponsible, destructive, or harmful to any living being or property. Freedom means obeying the nature of life, of being. It means *freedom through structure*. It means honoring the laws of a nation, a community, of a family, of every living being. Freedom is not being silenced. It is choice, it has a voice. Freedom is being the best loving person possible, leaving each moment as it passes better than when you entered it.

When you live by the law of freedom, you not only give freedom, but you are free. It involves letting go of preconceived ideas, ego programming, and agendas. Your mind and feelings are your equipment to live life. The Infinite cannot hurt itself, but an individual can and does when this law is broken.

Law of Balance

The law of balance is of utmost importance for your health, vitality, and well-being. The universal balance is so exact that when a grain of sand shifts, the whole world rebalances to adjust. To have a life of harmony, it requires a perfect balance in everything you do. Since you are a single focal point of Spirit, anything that you contribute to the well-being of life must come from within you. In other words, you must have something to give before you give it! That means it is essential that you take care of yourself first and then you have something to give to life, not the other way around. The first half is for you, the second half is for the world.

It is necessary to concentrate your attention on growth and unfoldment — to develop yourself to the best you can be. It is necessary to have courage, strength, health, wisdom, self-acceptance, or money to accomplish this giving. It is impossible to give what you don't have.

As a result of developing your individuality, you are able to serve, thereby fulfilling the second half, you bring balance to your life by giving service. If you serve with your hands, you must have the energy and vitality to follow through. If you are to serve with some kind of teaching, you have to educate yourself first. If you are to give money, you must have it before you can give it.

One of the major pitfalls to upset this law of balance is the do-gooder or martyrdom attitude. Are you doing something because you feel you have to, not because you want to? If you really don't want to loan someone money and you do, that is upsetting the law of balance for both of you. If you say "no" in the right place, through a natural law of attraction, that person will attract the one who needs to give the money. Both people prosper. If you can't give something freely, don't give it because it creates an imbalance in both of you. If a man is in trouble, your sympathy will do him no good. The only possible way you can help is by supporting with your strength. Sometimes that strength and wisdom is in the form of "no."

Some mothers martyr themselves by giving all to their families. What happens is that this kind of martyrdom creates a code of co-dependence and weakens everyone involved! The mother gives up her self-identity, and when motherhood is over, she feels empty and unfulfilled. The children leave home feeling guilt-ridden and appear to be selfish as they make their way in the world leaving mom behind. She disobeyed the law of balance — "First to self and second to the world." To return to wholeness, she has to become self-actualized. Self-reliant!

Find your natural rhythm — your own flow. It helps you to maintain balance in your lifestyle and to plan your life around your natural flow. Are you a morning person or a night person? When are you extroverted or introverted? When is your energy high or low? Do you like to work in solitude or are you a team player? This study allows you to maintain your ebb and flow — your rhythm!

You never lose anything that is for your highest good. Freedom and release are magnetic and keep a natural balance. The law of vacuum occurs when something goes out of your life, making room for something greater to move into your life. When a great love has left your life, that doesn't mean that no more love will come to you. All the Love of the universe is available — limitless, eternal, and inside of you!

This is why you release people, places, and things. If you hold on to your good too tightly, it keeps you out of balance and stops the flow. If you hold on to sand too tightly in your hand, you can't hold much. But if you hold it loosely, you can hold a lot more of it. By letting people move in and through your life, you never lose anything that is for your highest good. As something moves out, you'll develop a greater capacity to love, and someone or something or someplace will move in to develop and help you expand and accept a greater love. Love is growing. It forever becomes more expansive if you just let things go.

It's okay to get depressed or to be in a low state of mind. If this happens to you and someone tells you that you're not thinking properly because you are not having positive thoughts, it is not necessarily true. You could be releasing some old worn-out conditions so something new can move in. When you're depressed, accept the feeling and say, "So what, I'm just doing some emotional housecleaning. I'm releasing. I'm letting go. I'm making room for the new. This too shall pass. Vitality and balance are in my life now!"

By nonresistance, by not giving the depression any emotional power, by not getting into it and analyzing it, and by being detached from it, it will pass. And it moves into healing. If it's a relationship, it moves into harmony. If it's a situation, it moves into right action.

The art of complete relaxation is a secret power. The natural state of the body, emotions, and mind is to be rhythmic, which means to be active then passive, giving out then going back to the source to receive more intuitive energy. In that way you keep up a natural ebb and flow of life. It's absolutely necessary for the normal body. Release life, then relax. Release life, then relax. Do this all day long and you'll never be nervous or restrained. You have the proper tension to achieve that task at hand!

Perhaps you take yourself and others in your life too seriously. Learn to *detach yourself from people, places, and things*. When you are concerned, your attention and energy run out too far. You become uptight and anxious, thereby losing your balance and rhythmic vibration. Train yourself to relax and sink into the feeling of peace and joy and freedom, and you'll return to a positive state. Anything you resist, you give power to. Detach, release, let go. If there's a stagnant situation in your life, detach yourself from it. Become the observer. Affirm the positive and watch the negative disappear.

All of nature helps you to make it through this life. Nature is very loving. For example, you get the urge to go to the forest to rejuvenate. What happens when you sit under a tree is that the tree is just giving energy, and you're able to absorb this energy, revitalize, and get refreshed. Identifying with the rhythm of the ocean is very restful and refreshing. On the spiritual level, we are connected, energy to energy, in all forms. You have all of nature to nurture you with the healing power of love. In nature, love is given freely; the highest and finest and the best it can. It makes no decision about how much love it is going to give you. It simply gives love without conditions.

If you have a fruit tree in your yard, it doesn't say, "You haven't been very nice to me, so I'm not growing any leaves and the heck with fruit." It just gives its highest, finest, and best. Your pets — dogs, horses, cats — are very loving family members. One day I fell behind a car and I was knocked out. My friend was waiting in the car and didn't see what happened; so she didn't know I was in the car's path. Telepathically, the dog felt I was in danger, came tearing out of the house, and jumped upon my body. The dog gave me energy and I regained consciousness. I yelled at my friend so she knew not to back up. For a minute I felt angry at the dog for jumping on me. Suddenly I remembered this is how the energy system works. The dog was giving me energy to protect me, to bring me back to consciousness, which is a most loving action, and the love was given unconditionally. I was so grateful to my wondrous friend!

All of nature is telling you give, give, give. Don't analyze it, don't talk about it, don't think it out. Do it. Be it. Experience it. You no longer seek approval.

Ideas, not just physical bodies, solve problems. You have a mind, but you are more than mind. You have emotions, but you are more than emotions. You are Spirit. All powerful, all pervading, all wise, all knowing force, all loving force. You have the power of the universe right where you are.

An effective way to amplify the answer is to bless the quality that someone seems to lack. If you're in a negative situation, and let's say it's cooperation you need, unify with the perfect cooperation in you and the perfect cooperation in the other person or situation. If it's understanding you need, unify with that perfect understanding within yourself and within the other person. Whatever it is — wisdom, truth, freedom, love — unify with that within yourself and within them. It's an amazing healing power that is set in motion so you can enjoy a constructive situation.

What you mentally say *no* to departs easily, lovingly, and gently. You can say *no* in silence to some things, and when data starts to come in and you really don't quite know how to handle it, just say, "No. I do not accept this." You don't have to let everything into your space. You have a right not to be subjected to negativity.

If a friend whom you love is going through an organ recital, "My head aches … my throat is sore … my stomach aches … my back hurts … I have a sore leg." Instead of listening and sympathizing with your friend, don't play the game. You can still participate in the conversation by just saying, "Oh, no" or "Oh, really." What you're saying is, "No. That's not coming into my space." To say, 'Oh, really' is saying zero. You can also say in the silence of your mind, "No. I do not accept that. I affirm wholeness, health. Perfect head. Perfect throat. Perfect stomach. Perfect back. Perfect leg."

The word *no* declared in the conscious mind eliminates all incoming negativity. It is clear, direct, and to the point. Don't let the mind dwell on junk thoughts. Stop the idle random thinking, and stay focused on the task at hand. The subconscious mind really doesn't know the word *no*. It just says *yes* to everything! If you use an affirmation, "I am not a failure," your subconscious records this as "I am a failure." Be careful with your affirmations and be sure they are structured so you're verbalizing what you want, which in this case is "I am a success." Put your affirmations in the positive and the present tense, and use the word *no* to keep something out of your conscious mind. If someone you love is talking to you about problems, do not identify with the negatives by just saying in the silence, "No. I do not accept this." Add an affirmation to get your mind into the positive mode. Otherwise, there's a chance that you will absorb and get yourself congested. If the conversation continues long enough, you will have the ailment, the headache or stomachache or whatever. **If you don't say no, you are saying yes.** Your spiritual responsibility is to stand guard at the doorway of your mind and choose!

Emotional bonds are more subtle and tenacious than physical ones. To create new situations and to attract new people and things, you must loosen and let go of old relationships and old conditions. It is possible that something is blocking your acceptance of good as a result of your holding on to an emotional tie. In relationships, it is vital to reach a state of peace within yourself. You have to be on good terms with your past. If you are harboring negative feelings about the relationship on the subconscious level, you are still tied to that person. You are **not** responsible for the other person's well-being.

Use forgiveness and release to let go of those old ties. Even if a person has made a transition, he or she can still hang on to you. So you must release and let them go so they can get on with their growth in their new dimension, and you're free to experience a new relationship. It doesn't mean that there is any less love. It means that the love is more expanded, more inclusive.

Impulsiveness and Spontaneity

Impulsiveness and spontaneity take place on the emotional level (the feeling level). Impulsiveness is an emotional (thought plus feeling) response to an outer event or situation as an effect or programmed response. Spontaneity is an inner response to a feeling, or it can be called intuition or direct knowing or cause, and it is an appropriate response for right action in your life. Impulsiveness means reacting. Spontaneity means acting or action from within.

There is a big difference between acting and reacting, between spontaneity and impulsive behavior. Spontaneity is your intuitive direct knowing and comes from the Divine Intelligence within. Spontaneity and impulsiveness both involve change of plans. Impulsiveness is a result of outside information or person, place, or thing acting on you. It causes you to react, and the results are not always good. Sometimes they are and sometimes they're not. Impulsiveness involves a change of plans, but also involves an irresponsible change of plans. It means you are confused, and your action is based on emotional reaction instead of thinking decisively. Anytime you have to manipulate or force a plan of action, you know you are on a victim's pathway. When you are calm, spontaneity comes through the feelings as intuition. It only comes when you are relaxed into the proper tension, and it comes through feeling that can be interpreted mentally to make an appropriate choice. You feel comfortable with the action that follows even though it involves a change of plans, but it is right action and you feel good doing it with great results. Become more spontaneous in life so you are getting that flow of Intelligence that guides you in the here and now, consistently and continually. Never worry about the how or the end result — that is automatically taken care of since it is natural to move you into the direction of your life pathway easily, gently, and lovingly.

Spontaneity is intuition. Learn to trust your inner sixth sense. It is your spiritual guidance system from within and always leads you into your highest good.

Chapter Nine

Purpose, Goal Setting, and Decisions

Remember, your basic goal or purpose in life is to live, express and be yourself. To be yourself is the greatest thing you can do for yourself, your family, your country, the entire universe.

You are being and becoming either more of a person or less of a person every moment of your life. Change is one thing in this universe that you can depend on. Your goal should be one of being and becoming the Real You and to live and express the divine Spiritual Self. Meeting this goal also means to be self-reliant and self-actualized. This means revealing the true Real You and what you want to do and have and express, not what someone else has attempted to convince you that you should do, have, or express. There is an abundance in this universe, and you can have anything and everything that you can possibly desire. Your purpose for being and your duty to yourself and to the universe is to become a positive center, expressing the creative in Divine Timing, Divine Harmony, Divine Order, Divine Balance — or the Real You. As you develop this Spiritual Self, the higher are your vibrations and the more powerful you become as an individual.

Your Basic Purpose or Mission

Are you developing your potential? Are you accepting the negative appearances or the facts, or are you calling upon that higher knowledge, that all-wise answering device within you that will lead you through any situation to right action, to your true life path?

For a moment, think about your past. Looking back, you can see that everything that's happened to you made you grow. Didn't it shake you out of complacency and make you stretch? Life is full of challenges and changes, and you learn not to react to the point that you give up and get discouraged and become full of doubt and fear. When you get an understanding of Law and Love, you move through life easily, lovingly, and gently.

You'll find that every negative that comes is not really a negative. It's a challenge, an opportunity to bring out some of the true greatness within. You'll find you've got courage where you've never had it before. You've got talent in solving problems that is greater than you are. You're able to see through things. And as you meet these challenges one by one, you develop more empathy for others that are going through similar times, and you can take them by the hand and say, "You can make it."

If something happens to you, don't get discouraged. Just say, "Okay, this is fine. This too shall pass. This does not phase me. I'm in control. I can handle this by doing one thing at a time. One word. One thought. One moment." Sometimes life can get so adverse, that it takes all your strength and courage to handle it one moment at a time. Maybe you'll get to a point that you don't know which way to go or what to do. You're just there. All that's left is the blood circulating in your veins. Surrender to Spirit, to that all powerful Presence within. Let go and let God move through you, as you. You always have the answer when you have challenges. It's the way this process works. There's always a way if you just open up to it. Wait. Listen. Meditate.

From day to day, the subconscious mind guides you to what form of action is required in order to bring about the fulfillment of your dreams and desires. You receive this daily instruction in the form of urges and feelings. Your part is to respond with confidence and do whatever you are led to do.

All improvement is dependent upon seeing yourself as being greater than you now appear to yourself. When you realize there is a greater you seeking to express, then your potentials stir within you and your creative capabilities unfold. You are led in the right direction by your own Higher Self and you catch glimpses of the Real You.

Decisions

Every success-motivated mind has been a decisive mind. Every failure-motivated mind has been an indecisive mind. It takes as much hard mental work to fail as it does to succeed. Failure is actually a result of consistent negative patterns in the subconscious mind. Worry begets indecision, and indecision begets worry. Your decision, whether it is right or wrong, gives direction to your subconscious mind, and you are on your way to the end result.

Life responds to your decision with corresponding action. This is to say that the results you obtain or the demonstrations you make correspond with your ability to provide a mental acceptance of your desire. Once you have arrived at a decision, all the ideas that you need are revealed to you in the right order. Every important event in your life has taken place because of a decision made by you or made by someone else and accepted by you. Indecision is actually your decision to fail. Freedom of choice is your divine birthright. It remains your latent potential if you are an indecisive person.

You can always activate your potential. You were born to be the Real You. Your consciousness is fully equipped to express the Real You. All you have to do is wake up to that realization. If you cannot come to a decision to start being the Real You, then you continue to be a potpourri of other people's decisions. You continue to be a second-place person getting from life a small portion of the good that is possible.

Letting others make your decisions or leaning on the consciousness of others does not give you an opportunity to be what you can be. Eating three meals a day in a restaurant will never make you a gourmet cook. Not until you enter your own kitchen and use your own equipment will you start to cook. Your first results may not be inspiring, but at least you are now cooking. Be decisive, make the decision right now, to do your own decision making henceforth. Now you are cooking.

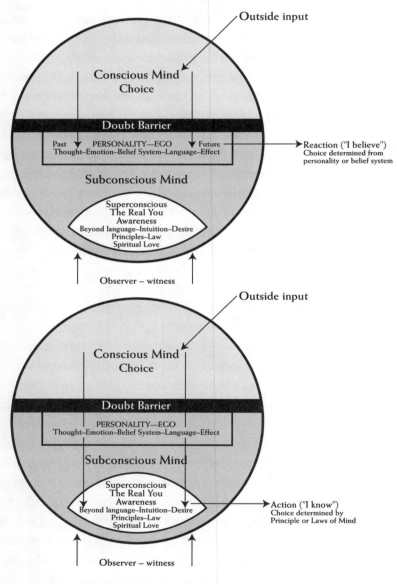

– Figure 13 –

THE ENERGY DYNAMICS OF A DECISION

When the conscious and the subconscious agree, you demonstrate.

(No attitudes, no opinions, no judgements or criticism)

You may say to yourself that you do not know what to do. At the center of your being, at the center of your mind, is the clear decision to be made. If you have a problem, you have an answer! Your thinking has caused the problem and your thinking can create the answer. It can be found instantly when your mind turns to the Divine Presence.

Why should you make your own decisions? You seek your own success and this success comes when you use your own resources. Every successful person is a success because of using ideas that came from within. Creative thinking does not come from another person. It happens in your own consciousness.

Fine ideas can be transmitted to you from others, but your original expression awaits your own self-discovery. Your unique way is already in your consciousness, for it was planted there in the beginning. You are spiritually designed to be a creative thinker. If you declare that you are a creative thinker, then interesting ideas come to your mind. Your ideas may not fit your usual patterns of thinking. In the beginning, they may make you uncomfortable, but do not reject them. This is Spirit beckoning you to areas of new success. These ideas are inviting you to become the explorer and the discoverer of new events. By this process, you seek the maturity of self-knowing, and you leave the immaturity of always seeking help or ideas from others.

Your conscious mind makes the decision and your subconscious mind acts upon the decision. One is the thinker and one is the doer (Figure 13). You do not control how your subconscious mind works, but you do control what you place into it by the decisions you make in accepting data or information. Your subconscious mind cannot refuse to serve you. The subconscious has no favorites and it has no limitation. You have the God-given ability and right to demand that the subconscious act.

Goals

The establishment of goals is the conscious decision of the conscious mind. If you have no real goals, then I challenge you to get specific about a goal. The word goals is taunting, challenging, or

– Figure 14 –

HOW DO I CHOOSE A GOAL?

1. **What do I desire?**

2. **Why don't I have it now?**

3. **What are the obstacles?** (In every obstacle lies the key to another level of awareness.)

4. **How do I overcome these?** (Plan of action...start with a mental plan.) (Spiritual mind treatment)

5. **Is it really worth it?**

> Self-acceptance is your regulator. Both positive and negative thinking are reactive thinking; neutral thinking is balanced thinking.

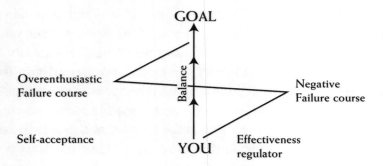

1. **Do you really want to succeed?**

2. **Direction of thought** — Are you going to, rather than coming from?

distasteful to many. The aged excuse themselves by saying it's too late. The young complain that they have no chance and no one listens to them. The middle-aged state their limited aims and think they are sufficient.

Think in great terms. I dare you! Dream a great dream. I challenge you to do this. Nothing is impossible to those who decide that it is possible. The universe responds to you and your thought or decision by corresponding and by becoming the thing that you have determined shall come into being. The framework or opinions are the only limitations set upon you. These limitations are subject to change at a moment's notice and that moment's notice is when you consciously decide and make the decision to make the change. A directed mind is a healthy mind.

There are six questions to ask yourself to validate a goal (Figure 14). Write down the answers so you can study them.

What do I desire? This does not mean what do I want for my children, my spouse, my friends. What does the Real Me desire? Not what I should have, ought to have, or must have. This takes truthfulness.

Why don't I have it now? Maybe you'll say time, finances, a relationship, talent, and so on.

What are the obstacles? You may say money is an obstacle. If you've got a money problem, you don't really have a problem. Money can always be obtained because you live in an abundant universe. It's a matter of changing your thought patterns of lack and limitation and getting those patterns straightened out and healed. It's a matter of realigning your priorities. Ideas set up a law of attraction and magnetically draw to you the means by which to manifest those ideas.

How do I overcome these? Start with a mental plan of action. You treat for guidance. You speak your word for immediate cash if that's the problem. You speak your word for the right ideas, for the right people, for right action. *What the mind can conceive, the mind can achieve. Principle is not set by precedent.* Just because society has said there's only one way to do something doesn't make it true. With a deeper understanding of the laws of physics or the natural laws, many new ways evolve from the old

belief systems. Don't get caught up with what has been done —
there is always a way to overcome the obvious. Don't let anyone
take your dream away from you. Part of overcoming an obstacle
is not to discuss your goals with other people. Be silent, steady,
and true to your treatment or to your goal so you don't dissipate
the energy on the way. If you're going to talk about it, talk about
it with people who will help you take the next step, not people
who are inclined to say, "Oh, why do you think like that? You're
so silly. You're off in your dream world again." Many dreams
have been destroyed by that kind of discussion, especially the
dreams of children.

When you have a dream or a goal, you get excited and enthusiastic about it, and there is a tendency to talk about it without
ceasing. With every word you speak, you move the energy
away; you dissipate the Power. If you want to use that energy to
develop the pattern that you're building within you, be quiet so
it can gather more energy and draw to it that which it needs to
manifest into your life magnetically.

Overcome obstacles with a plan of action. If you get stopped
physically, mentally, or emotionally, clear your mind. Do what
you can each day to be true to your goal without force or manipulation, then focus on the task at hand. Surrender the goal to
your Higher Power when there's a block. Continue with the task
at hand and the pathway clears. It works!

What are the rewards to me personally if I get my desire? If there
are no benefits in your goal for you, you do not have a valid
goal. You may say, "I want this money to help people and save
the world. I'm going to do good with it. That's why I'm working
for money. I don't want any of it for myself." That's a myth. People say, "I'm doing this for my children." That is not a valid
goal, that's sacrifice. It will harm you as well as the children. By
taking care of yourself, you are able to take care of your respon-
sibilities as a parent.

There's got to be a reward in it for you. If it benefits you, then
it will benefit others automatically. You may ask, "Why do I
have to pay income taxes?" You don't have to pay taxes, but it's
worth it to you if you like living in the United States of America.

In essence, what you're saying is, "I want to pay taxes because of the benefits I receive." Even though there may be many things that need healing in America, it's still the most efficient system in the world, and it gives the most freedom for individuals. So it's a privilege to pay income taxes. You pay taxes because of the benefits you receive.

Avoidance and denial of the payment of taxes takes you out of a capitalistic system. If you decide not to pay taxes, you are also deciding not to prosper. It is important to realize that the two go together! The law of reflection responds to your denial by denying you your good. It is that simple. Enjoy being part of a financial system that does work!

This is also why you do things for your children. It's not because you have to; it's because you want to for the benefits you receive. Sometimes parents feel sorry for themselves because they haul their kids here and there. Taking a deeper look at the situation, they are saying, "I want to do this because of the joy it gives me seeing my children express better. I'm giving them an opportunity to grow." The parents, then, are doing it for themselves, not for their children.

You can change your attitude towards your mundane tasks, for example, doing dishes because of a sense of well-being and order around you. You don't have to like doing the dishes, but you do like the benefits you receive. There has to be a personal reward in everything you do.

Is it really worth it? You may decide that a lot of your goals are not valid, that they are not worth it for the stress and the strain, the treatment, and the mental work it's going to take to do it. There must be something better for you.

If you don't know what your life work is, you certainly know one thing — you are here to be and become yourself. An affirmation for discovering your life work is, "Divine Wisdom reveals to me my true life's work. I am now guided, guarded, and protected into right action to achieve this."

Once your goal is established in your mind, the perfect pathway to the goal is through divine order, divine harmony, divine timing, divine balance, divine rhythm. This means that you move toward your goal in perfect unfoldment and perfect ful-fillment. You go forward easily, lovingly, and gently with all your needs met.

Let's say that you are on your pathway, and suddenly you find yourself in the unknown, in a state of confusion or doubt or fear. You are aware then that you're on a negative course, and you have to decide whether to get back on course or not. If you continue on this course of failure, you aren't going to reach your goal because you're getting bogged down in negativity. Take the time to meditate, to affirm, to speak your word, to bless the Divine in yourself and in whatever else needs to be divinely blessed, and get yourself back on the track.

Perhaps you do a super job and you feel really enthusiastic. You're excited and stimulated beyond belief. You're so stimu-lated, you're so hyper, overexcited, and so enthusiastic that you get yourself out of balance. This is just as much a failure course as the negative one was.

Be centered, calm, serene, and allow yourself an easy flow of energy and intelligence and proper tension for the body. Many times a sales course can be very stimulating and when you leave five minutes later, you fall flat, flatter than you've ever been. It's due to over stimulation. In Western society, the ego demands stimulation and demands almost hyper-action, dramatic change. This is why there are so many cases of ulcers, migraine headaches, and heart attacks in our society. The tendency is to feel as though nothing's happening if it comes too easily, quietly, lov-ingly, and gently. This is not the truth!

The thing that affects your effectiveness regulator is how you feel about yourself, your acceptance of self. When you find yourself in the failure or over-stimulation course, check out your self-acceptance. Are you trying to force action? Are you trying to pretend something that you're not feeling? Examine your con-sciousness — look for any doubts or fears that may be trying to surface. Refocus and put yourself on course again.

Here are some questions you need to ask yourself. Do you really want to succeed? Maybe that's someone else's idea for you. Society tends to tell you are not really successful unless you have all monetary benefits. That's not true. There are many ways to be successful. Only you know what that is for you. Perhaps someone has told you that you cannot succeed, and you have a pattern of almost being successful, but not quite. Look at the feedback you get from the subconscious mind and identify who is controlling and pushing your success button — is it a school teacher? is it a college professor? is it your mother and/or your father? a friend? someone who has put you down, taken your dream and torn it to shreds? Maybe when you were five years old, you were given a spanking and told you that you were a real failure. The message may have been very subtle — you were in a world of adults who seemed to ignore you, and you always felt you had to reach so far and never quite made it. Sometimes you don't know the root of this thought pattern, but break through it now. See it for what it is. Work your way through the doubt and fear. Accept your truth, accept your Spiritual Self — whole, complete, all of the love there is. Right now!

In the success mechanism, you are always moving in a direction. You're either going towards your goal or you're moving away from it. This requires daily checks of "where am I in thought?" You can be negative in thought. In which direction are your thoughts taking you? Thought directs the energy. You build your life, word by word and thought by thought, all day long.

Definite plans bring definite results. A decisive person is a successful person. Once you have chosen your goal, it is easier to make decisions. Mentally embody your goal or your treatment. In your mind, you act as if you already have the goal or already have it completed. Experience it in feeling and emotion as being done and complete. This doesn't mean that if you are treating for a million dollars, you act as if the money is there and start writing checks. Instead, you feel and act as if you are a millionaire. Work with this at the level of your acceptance until you really know it and can trust it. You have then embodied your treatment. When you experience it in your imagination as being done or completed, you *know* that you know!

Get a mental equivalent. If you are treating for a car and your goal it to have this beautiful car for a certain vacation, go ahead and pack your bag to go on the trip with your new car. That is symbolic of accomplishing your goal of already having the car. Maybe you can go buy a new pair of gloves to drive your new car. Embodying the car means acting "as if," and driving it in your imagination. Mental embodiment means building a car consciousness — embodying the idea of owning a car. You can also make a treasure map or put together a scrap book or put ideas down on paper — all of this helps you embody the ideas. If it's a home you want, get samples of paint and carpeting and put them on your treasure map. Don't get into price or get into how you'll get it. Get pictures of what you desire that would be an equivalent of what you want to experience.

Visualization

Imagery, visualization, is a powerful tool. It can be used effectively in completing an idea in mind. There are two basic exercises of imagery to practice. One method is keeping your mind focused on the completed idea (when you know what you want). Let images and ideas come and go until the picture is exactly what you want, and then release it to the subconscious. The second method is for when you don't have a clear idea about what you want. Keep a pen and paper handy as you let ideas float in and out of your mind. Finally, an image will keep appearing, and it is usually the answer you were looking for. Always see yourself participating in some way in the visualizations. Some people have difficulty using imagery because they see things in words. Actually, all thought comes in pictures in the mind, it is just a matter of how it is interpreted that makes the difference. Time the exercises to about fifteen minutes so you don't end up just daydreaming or fantasizing. Always put yourself in the center of the picture. Otherwise, it comes all around you, but you don't get to enjoy it. It is vital to be precise in your picturing.

Visualize and think in terms of success. If your goal is to succeed and you're preparing for failure, there is something inconsistent in your behavior. For example, you are treating for a new wardrobe, but you are holding onto old things in your closet in preparation for a depression by saying, "Maybe I'll need that."

Clean out your closet and prepare for the new. If you haven't worn something in the past six months or the last year, get rid of it unless you know it is of value to you. If it's creating an image or thought of lack and limitation, release it to someone else.

If you have a lot of hobby-related items around and you are not using them, clean them out. Let's say you like to sew, and you gather fabric that fills all your closets. Every time you look at the fabric you say, "I'm going to sew some day." That is a negative energy, and it will drain you every time you look at it because it is reminding you of failure and of guilt for not completing the project.

Look around your home and see what you have that is putting a subtle subconscious pressure on you. Then get rid of it and anything that reminds you of lack. If lack of prosperity is standing in the way of your success, get rid of all confusion in your home. Clean out drawers. Establish order around you. Divine order is definitely related to prosperity. When you clean out drawers and closets and create order, it brings you into the right mental image and sends a message to the subconscious mind to create flow.

It is important that you coordinate the thing you desire with what you are picturing. Let's say you are treating for a new car, perhaps a Mercedes Benz, and every time you treat for a Mercedes, you picture a truck in your mind because you think that's all you can afford. A truck is what you are going to get because that's what you're imaging. Make sure your desire and your visualization are matched.

Perhaps your goal is to be slender and elegant, and every time you think thin, fat pops in your mind. You're defeating your goal. You will produce fat. It is a good idea to stop thinking of fat and thin and start working toward achieving a healthy lifestyle and think of eating for vital energy. Think in terms of health, and then there is no negative feedback from the subconscious mind.

Look at the words and thoughts you are working with and see what kind of feedback you are getting. You may have to change the wording so that your desire and your imagination are working together. What you picture in mind and accept in consciousness is what is demonstrated in your outer world.

Move your consciousness into a totally new territory where there can be no argument from the subconscious mind. Say to yourself, "I'm better today in every way." There is no argument with that. Then every day you are guided into right action or you move into a greater awareness of what is right action. If you want to quit smoking, you don't deal with it by saying, "I want to quit smoking." You begin to think of ways to keep your hands busy. You begin knowing that your energy is now being used in appropriate and beautiful ways to take you to a greater fulfillment and unfoldment of the truth of you. Perhaps you are guided to paint a picture or to start working in the garden, using your hands for good instead of holding a cigarette.

Being overweight or lack and limitation are results of the misuse and misdirection of energy. Sometimes you are indecisive, scattered, confused, blocked, and you find it difficult to meditate or be true to your goal. It's because the natural flow of your energy is not being directed in the right way. Energy has to go somewhere, and that's why it sometimes manifests on the body as fat. It has everything to do with your emotional and mental attitude towards yourself, to some thought patterns that are creating the negative experience. To move into healthful living, you need to work with the mental and emotional as well as the physical levels in order to get results that last.

Many times on the way to achieving a goal, you are hampered by programming on the subconscious level. That's really what you're working on — fear patterns, success patterns, acceptance of good, a sense of worthiness, and working with the idea that you are a totally self-contained unit. Don't underrate yourself or your potential. You came into this life totally self-contained, and you have everything you need to be and become. Work with your self-acceptance.

Take long-range goals and divide them into short periods of time. Take a step every day, and say to yourself, "What definite and specific thing can I do today to achieve my goal?" Success represents a lot of little steps, not big leaps. It's a lot of little decisions made when working toward the goal. It is working with a sense of well-being every day. At the end of every day, pat yourself on the back — number one, for making it through alive; second, for the good that happened that day; third, for your ability to cope. Find something good that happened to you, and give thanks for it.

The 7 C's

You can use the seven C's, clarity, cleansing, continuity, coordination, completion, commitment, and creativity (Figure 15), to keep you on track with your goal.

1. *Clarity*. Be decisive with a clear focus.
2. *Cleansing*. Create a vacuum and release old worn-out conditions to make room for the new.
3. *Continuity*. In a state of oneness, keep on with the task at hand with concentration. All actions lead to the goal.
4. *Coordination*. Keep things orderly with effective planning and prioritizing.
5. *Completion*. Finish the task at hand. It is an important message to the subconscious to complete before moving on to the next task. It eliminates confusion and loose ends.
6. *Commitment*. Discipline yourself to stay on the course because of the benefits you receive by achieving your goal.
7. *Creativity*. A focused mind is centered and draws power to the present. Intuition is sharpened and ideas flow. You are doing things in your unique way and trusting yourself to accomplish the desired results.

If you are in a place where you are affecting others, have an attitude of cooperation and communication. Never get intimidated by an authority figure. No one is greater than you. Everyone around you represents a part of you. Each is a reflection of you. Everyone in your experience comes to you through the law of attraction. Nothing happens by accident or coincidence. You

– Figure 15 –

THE 7 C'S

CLARITY
DEFINITE PLANS BRING DEFINITE RESULTS. DECISIONS.

CLEANSING
CREATING A VACUUM, MAKING ROOM FOR THE NEW. RELEASING.

CONTINUITY
FOLLOW THROUGH, CONCENTRATION, FOCUS.

COORDINATION
PLANNING, ARRANGING, ORDER, AND PRIORITIZING.

COMPLETION
FINISHING THE TASK AT HAND, ONENESS.

COMMITMENT
DISCIPLINE TO LAW AND LOVE. LIVING THE PRINCIPLES.

CREATIVITY
DOING IT YOUR WAY, UNIQUENESS.

don't have to be subjected to negativity. Handle the situation with love and self-integrity and leave when quality energy changes to negativity.

Authority and leadership are two different modes of behavior. Authority comes from an external force acting upon you. It is coercing and manipulating you into action through intimidation. Leadership is inspiration from within. Leadership encourages the creativity of the individual and creates an atmosphere of security and encouragement to express.

If people around you seem to have a greater talent or more power, remember that what is around you is you, and you are greater than the sum total of the parts. If you keep that in mind, you won't get hung up on labels like boss or executive, king, or queen. The door to honest and real communication is opened when you are not intimidated by labels or opinions. Occasionally it is necessary to have a confrontation with an authority figure to keep the balance. It may help both of you and be a growing experience. Blessing the Truth of the situation, use the "I" messages — "I feel I must say this … This is my experience …." Set a time aside and talk to your boss; don't walk away from it. Call, make it official, and set up a conference. Have things written down. It will help you keep from becoming emotional. State your causes and ask for a change of behavior, then be silent. Don't be afraid of silence. It can be your greatest friend. Let your boss think about your points. If there is just silence, it can be an opportunity for both of you to grow. You won't get fired unless you want to be. You hire and fire yourself in consciousness. It can be such a relief to both of you to have these issues brought up and discussed that you could probably get a raise and be considered for a promotion in the future because of your wisdom and forthrightness.

It is important to efficiently use your time while moving towards your goals. Do the thing and the Power is there! Begin now where you are. This leaves no room for procrastination. If you procrastinate, you are putting off the task at hand. Just get into it and focus on it. If it is a monotonous, mundane chore, putting it aside doesn't get rid of it. Unify with the Power and Presence and think Oneness. It makes you more efficient and more effective in what you're doing. As you center within Spirit, what previously took you six hours can now take you one hour. Procrastination is a failure mechanism. It is important to complete an action!

Rationalizing is another failure mechanism. If you spend your time trying to logically think everything out, you're already in the past. Reading body language and things like that are helpful if you're a mentalist, but you're far more. You are recognizing that you have all the information within. While you're reading everybody's body signals, you're missing your intuitive direct knowing messages. Move past the physical. When you are working with your astrology chart, you're already missing the vibration of the new movements of the stars. These are effects to which you are giving power. When you make a decision by using the outer effect, it is done by rationalizing, by explaining, or by analyzing the effect. This puts you out of timing and out of synchronicity with your real Self. This blocks the direct intuitive answers from within that are relevant to the now. Now is all there is! Live the present moment directed from within without recycling the past and rehashing people's opinions. Work from the inner self (cause) to the outer experience. Cause creates an effect.

Recognize that changes take place at the level of your acceptance. You may analyze for a while. Maybe you need to study yourself to see where you really are in thought and emotions. As soon as you can, get established in the here and now and trust that inner spontaneity to take you where you belong. If you're centered in your right place, everything you need is there. Most explanations are a cop-out anyway, and they dissipate your power.

Get effective with the word no. Suppose someone you love calls you up to take you to lunch. You really don't want to go and you don't want to hurt feelings. Realize you cannot hurt someone unless they want to be hurt. It is their choice. Let them be responsible for their reactions. Develop the ability to say "no" without explaining. Explanations waste everyone's time.

The basic premise behind this is that you do not seek approval. You do your thing. You let it go. The approval is automatic.

(Harmony is a natural state of being.) If you're being true to yourself and true to your space, you're not being selfish. You are being good and loving to everybody by being honest, and you are allowing right action to take care of the situation. In other words, you have made room for the right person to be there for lunch. It creates a more direct communication, an atmosphere of answers instead of confusion.

Discourage interruptions. Answer the door or the telephone only when it's convenient. Do what feels right action to you. Bless the good in yourself and the good in the person at the door, then ignore that knock and get on with your work. A test to see if you're being honest with yourself is to let the phone ring three times before you move a muscle to answer it. Observe your body tense up. It's amazing how people respond to bells — doorbells, school bells, telephones, whistles. Give yourself permission to move and take control over the energy, and don't be intimidated by a bell. Do it on your terms and practice proper tension so you aren't rushing because you think you're going to miss something. You are always in your right place at the right time in the right way, and any information that is relevant will come to you. Maybe if you answered the telephone, it would put you out of synchronicity with what needs to be done to keep in flow, therefore creating stress. Release it to its greater good. If it's information that's important to you, it will come to you. You always get the information you need in time to proceed in right action. Even if it is of a tragedy, you're going to get the information soon enough to take care of the details. If you get it too soon, you're not emotionally prepared. Trust that you're always in your right place at the right time, in the right way to handle any situation in the most stable manner.

Make productive use of time while you wait for people. Carry a book with you, or if you don't have a book, observe where you are. Become an observer. Perhaps you're in an atrium or a garden, and just enjoy the flowers and plants. Identifying with nature can energize you. Accept where you are and don't let someone irritate you because they don't seem to be in their right place at their right time. There are people who are consistently late. If you get upset over that, they have exerted control over you by getting you to react, therefore, you become the victim.

Another technique to help you move out of old habit patterns or ruts that are keeping you from achieving your success is to change your routines. Drive to work a different way every day. Instead of serving a roast and potatoes for dinner, serve it for breakfast. Give no explanation. Stay up all night and sleep all day. Watch and see how regimented you are; get out of your comfort zone for a while. Change jobs for a day with your partner. If you hate cooking, eat out. See how you are controlled by regimented ideas. Change can bring a new dimension to your life. It is vital to your flow to remain flexible and spontaneous.

If you're playing the role of Perfect Mother and you are exhausted, quit. It's time to delegate, negotiate tasks, plan and prioritize the family group. Teach order, self-reliance and responsibility. Change the way you do things. Create an atmosphere of cooperation and love.

Look at the routines you're involved in every day and see what you're repeating like a broken record. You may be dealing with worn-out conditions like the mother, who for several years cooks for five people, and then there are only two. Yet every week she continues to buy groceries for five and cooks heavy meals. Change old patterns and routines that are no longer consistent with where you are now in your growth and development.

Keep in mind that *no one is your enemy and no one is your friend. Everyone is your teacher.* Remembering this gives you a new perspective regarding the people in your life and helps you to mentally stay open to learning new things about yourself.

Often you are in denial about what really is going on in your life. One clue is that you do not feel fulfilled. Are you afraid of greatness or afraid to face change? Are you afraid to be successful?

Accept where you are without criticism and let the Higher Self, the Real You, lead you gently through the subconscious negative self to the spiritual pathway. The Higher Self is that part of you that is beyond the mind, beyond thought, reason, or logic. It is something within you that is all-powerful, ever-available, all-wise, ever-constant, waiting upon you to open up to It and recognize the Power and Presence that is within you. It leads, guides, and protects you into right action in your life at this moment!

There are no two people alike. You have a unique place in this universal plan. There is a Divine Pattern within you now. If you're having difficulty connecting with this Self, here is an affirmation that can help you reveal the Power within. Whatever you desire, believe you have it and say to yourself, "I surrender all fear, all doubt. I let go of all uncertainty. I am wise and clear and I have confidence. What belongs to me comes to me. I stake my claim. It is revealed to me now, and I accept it. I accept the gift of Life. Now I function and flow in the Divine and experience true joy."

Chapter Ten

Prosperity

You are a totally self-contained unit of the creative life energy; therefore, you have, right now, the power and patterns within you for unlimited prosperity at the level of your acceptance. Prosperity represents more a way of life than having a large bank account. Being rich is the ability to do what you want to do in the way you want to do it. Right now! An element of wealth is not in having things, but in handling things.

The more self-esteem and self-acceptance you have, the more willing you are to trust yourself and follow your intuition, the more money you will have. It has been said that confidence doubles your power and multiplies your abilities. Lack and limitations merely mirror the energy blocks and congestion in your consciousness. The more you release the ego's hold on you and the more you trust your inner guidance, the more wealth increasingly flows into your life. These manifestations come easily, gently, and effortlessly in a joyful way without sacrifice.

Here are some ideas and thoughts that create blocks to your flow:

- Keeping your focus centered in the future and not taking care of the now.
- Waiting until everything is perfect before acting on an urge, or refusing to take risks.
- Holding back on life by being indecisive. All of these take you out of synchronicity.

Your belief system may be effecting you more than you realize.

- You hold a belief that money is dirty or evil or feel an ambivalence about money. Part of you rejects it, and part of you resents not having it. The universe takes you at your word, and so your finances fluctuate. It comes and goes. This results because there is no consistency in your thinking, so there is no consistency in your finances.

You may always be wanting something in your conversation, and the very fact that you want keeps the very thing away from you. The universal law obeys and you will keep on wanting.

It is up to you to accept and then you have what you desire. Give up the word want and say, "I have" or "I accept now" or "I desire."

- The myth of scarcity may be the underlying theme of your whole belief system, e.g. "I don't have enough time" or "I don't have enough sleep" or "I don't have enough talent" or enough friends; and on and on it can go. No matter what is happening, your theme is, "It is not enough" and finally, "I am not enough." The tendency is to have others agree, "There just isn't enough."

- If you have old parent tapes running through your mind, you may have to give yourself permission to prosper. It may be your child in your consciousness that keeps you obeying the old parent tapes — that you don't deserve to prosper. Give yourself permission to be wealthy! Change the old boundaries, open up to include more in your life.

- What thoughts or attitudes in you are repelling your wealth? Do you deny others their good? Do you spread rumors about lying and cheating, gossiping about others' wealth or good? Accusation, denial of others' good all come home to you and become your experience. Every word that leaves your mouth comes back to you multiplied. Give up judgements and criticism of anything or anyone, including yourself. You may find yourself fearing wealthy people or resenting them. Are you blaming someone else for your lack? Do you feel like punishing people because they are not giving you what you deserve? Discern, instead, what that particular person or situation means to you. What does this meaning reveal about your own consciousness? Remember, you created your universe.

If you don't like it, change your attitude to one of good and positive growth.

When you are going through challenging times, it is better to be still about your lack or financial disasters and talk more about your visions and dreams. Instead of complaining or whining about what's going wrong, talk of something that is positive in your life.

- To experience prosperity, this theme has to be changed to one of limitlessness of the universe, the wholeness and completeness of this natural system. Abundance and prosperity are everywhere, and it is your birthright to be prosperous. It is natural.
- If you find yourself in a temporary cash flow challenge, it may be that Spirit is guiding you and keeping you from doing something foolish. Remember, you are always in the right place, right now, in the right way for your good. There is no denial in Spirit.

7 Steps to Prosperity

1. *Focus.* The key to focus is to concentrate on one thing at a time. In this way, you become more efficient and effective in anything you do. Practice the oneness of mind in the now. Pay attention to what you are doing right now. Be totally present! Complete each task at hand to the degree you can without force or coercion. This creates clarity and cohesiveness to your day. Your energies are not scattered all over the place, which causes confusion.

The power of concentration also opens up your intuitive abilities, which continually support you with guidance and answers. It allows the proper tension for the task at hand, and the spiritual energy continues to flow in support. You stop this flow when you are stressed or uptight. Spirit does not force Itself upon you, so it is important to have a detached and relaxed attitude at all times. The more specific you are about your desire, the more definite the answers or demonstrations are. Never get into *how* it happens. Focus on answers rather than on the problem. This does not mean you ignore the problem, but rather you quickly review the facts and move your attention to the answer. Stay with what is right in this situation rather than with what is wrong with it.

2. *Divine Order.* Create order in your life — mentally, emotionally, physically, and socially. Make the decision necessary to create flow. Get rid of any excess to create room for the new. You must be decisive — sitting on the fence blocks your flow.

Procrastination is a decision to fail. Be a do-it-now person. As soon as you can, get rid of credit cards. Keep one and pay it immediately when it is due. Any delay means your good is delayed in coming to you. When you're late with your payments, you're late with your demonstration. This is one way to develop a good credit history. Don't spend what you don't have, don't rob Peter to pay Paul. This means you do not take cash from the credit card to pay other debts. Keep order all around you, do the dishes, keep the garage cleaned out, the laundry washed, folded and put away, make your bed in the morning, pick up your clothes and put them away in the closet, keep the yard neat and tidy, your desk orderly. All of this reminds the subconscious of completion. The act of completion sends a very strong message to the subconscious. An unfinished task signals a negative message and represents one of failure to the subconscious.

3. *Vacuum.* For a change of consciousness, make a change in mind first to make room for the new. Release relationships that have completed. Get rid of people who create chaos and usurp your time. It is important to release possessive clinging to other people in your life. Through possessive emotional ties, the energy of your thoughts and feelings are directed into their life, which you could be using in your own. Also, dominating or controlling another person causes distraction. You lose concentration and focus when this takes place and depletion occurs. Release worn-out conditions and completed situations from the past to open up to the new. That means releasing clothes you no longer wear, furniture that crowds a room, and anything that reminds you of lack or poverty, like saving something unnecessarily, in case you might need it someday.

4. *Visualization*. In your use of visualization, see everything completed, as the end result. Do not get into outlining how it is going to happen; that task belongs to the subconscious to perform, and how it does it is still to this day, a mystery. But it does do it, and on that you can depend! Always include yourself in the picture or you will be on the outside looking in at your demonstration. Image yourself receiving or living your good now, feeling wonderful and joyful in your new life. Create a vision of wealth and prosperity, and soon the world reflects that back to you. Through imaging, you can eliminate any blocks or impurities, such as envy, fear, worry, and coveting another's wealth. All of your attention goes to the complete picture of already having your desire and the joy that it brings.

5. *Magnetism*. This technique energizes everything with blessing, praising, and giving thanks. Bless everything that leaves your life to its greater good and know that all good will be returned to you. When you pay your bills, bless the check or cash and know that what you bless increases and is returned to you multiplied. When you have a temporary budget breakdown or cash flow challenge, put all your bills in a basket. Bless them all and give thanks for the service rendered when you needed it, and know the same force that brought you the service will bring you the means to pay for it. By doing this, you are actually paying the bill first spiritually. This is very, very powerful!

The feeling of magnetism is one of the major tools for acquiring wealth. You start by embodying the essence of what it is you want. You energize the images with all your senses. In your imagination, touch it, taste it, see it, smell it, and hear it. Imbue your image with all the emotional, mental, and spiritual energy you can bring forth. It magnetizes the image and sets up the law of attraction which will bring it right to you. There is no force used. If you have to apply too much power, you are probably going against the current of your natural flow. Learn to harmonize with the energy.

If your idea is to have a larger amount of money, make sure you're comfortable with that amount of money. Observe closely how you are feeling and imagine how your lifestyle would be different. This should bring out any hidden fears that may be blocking you from having more money. Does it mean you have to give up the privacy which you now enjoy? Can you handle the responsibility of having large amounts of money by hiring accountants, lawyers, and bankers? Do you fear the taxes that you might have to pay?

Work with the image until you feel an inner knowing that all is well — until you can say, "Yes, this is mine. It is good and I can handle it easily, lovingly, and gently." Then let it go! You have mentally, emotionally, and spiritually embodied your desire. It is done unto you as you believe.

6. *Acceptance*. You accept everything first on the mental level and you see it as being done. Establish a mental equivalent of having accepted your desire. For example, if you are desiring a new car, buy a pair of gloves with which to drive this new car. Get something symbolic that represents the acceptance of your desire as already being completed. If it's a vacation, get a poster of the destination, and go ahead and pack your bags.

Build an appreciation of all things, people, and places, that represent prosperity to you. (This helps build a new conscious-ness of wealth.) There is no *hard* or *easy* or *big* and *little* in the Divine Intelligence; there is only big and little in your mind. You are developing capacity and expansion in your aura. What the mind can conceive, you can achieve. Unlimited thinking can be achieved by changing old boundaries to include more. After you have accepted your desire, your inner guidance leads you in the simplest, most effortless way possible. It is up to you to listen and follow the natural flow of energy to achieve that desire.

7. *Thanksgiving and tithing*. Build an attitude of daily grati-tude. It sets up the magnetic law of attraction that keeps your good flowing. Tithe ten percent of your net income to a *spiritual account* to give back to life — maybe it's your life that you can contribute to for your spiritual growth. It works!

Giving and receiving are a part of thanksgiving. Give only whatever you can from the heart. Your gift is not a gift when you feel obligated or forced to give. Any feelings of reluctance or lack are a sign that the giving is not for the highest good. Give only what you can with no strings attached. Giving is not for what you can get back. Be aware when you give money so you do not create a dependency — the purpose of life is to become self-reliant.

Receiving sometimes is the most difficult. Most of us find it easy to give, but cannot receive graciously. Remember, it is the universe giving to you and you owe nothing. Of course, you have not received when you feel an obligation to pay back. The gift of obligation hurts you, and the one attempting to be generous. If there is a feeling of obligation, it is best you not receive the gift. Be open and receptive to all the gifts Spirit has to give you — health, joy, wholeness, well-being, companionship, and on and on. Life has much to offer if you are willing to receive. Open up your heart and mind and live the life of all good.

Give thanks for your unexpected good coming from unexpected places in unexpected ways (not the known ones). Appreciation is a state of mind that sets up the laws of attraction and brings more prosperity.

Your plan can also include a mental plan of action, a Spiritual Mind Treatment, which is basically speaking your word or verbalizing your desire as being here now. An example is: "The Universe is prosperous and abundant. I am the center of this Prosperity Pattern. I now speak my word and accept, easily, gently, and lovingly, a divine increase in all my financial sources, known and unknown. All my desires are fulfilled. I am amply rewarded for services rendered. I prosper in everything I do. I am grateful. And so it is." Now release this treatment and move into action, into doing the things you know to do to achieve your desire without force, manipulation, or coercion. Treat and move your feet!

Chapter Eleven

The Spiritual Self — The Real You

The spiritual level of your identity is the Real You. It is the Spiritual Self. Within you is the spiritual source of your individuality which contains a knowingness, perfect wisdom, an awareness that is beyond thought. Thought is thinking about something; awareness is being there! This part of your identity is unlike anything you have ever thought. You may have had glimpses of It because It has always been there. You do not create this portion of your individuality by thought, It is a Power and Presence which is already within you, all around you, and within every person, place, and thing. It is the Life Energy in form. It is the invisible Power and Pattern made visible.

Your Real Self is a unique individualization of the creative process which is always producing more of what It is. You are a being that is always becoming. This Real You, this Spiritual Self, is completely unaware of anything unlike Itself, for It is all-powerful, all-knowing, and ever-present. This level of your Self is beyond reason and logic, for It is experienced as a feeling. You can ignore this portion of yourself, and It does not impose Itself upon you. Or you may turn to It as a Power and Presence in Life, and It is always there to guide, guard, and protect you when you are relaxed into the proper tension for the task at hand in the now.

It is that something within, like the oak tree that is within the acorn. You cannot see it, yet you can experience its essence. You know It's there. It is that Intelligence within you that is beyond time and space. It has no beginning and no end. It has no language. It is beyond good and bad or duality. It is simple. It is Oneness. It is the eternal now. Spirit knows no past or future.

It has no limits. It's impersonal. It's Pure Essence or Pure Love. It never says *no* to you. It always says, *yes*. You cannot destroy It. It's always there. It's the resident within every cell of your being, within every tissue and organ of your structure, and It is all around you. It's in you, above you, below you. It surrounds you. It's yours to use. All you have to do is turn to It, and because It functions as law, if you use It with love, you build a constructive life — word by word, thought by thought, deed by deed. The law only knows to do!

Self-Integrity and Sensitivity

If you begin to see this as the hidden cause within everything, you experience the connecting link that leads you to develop a unity consciousness, realizing the oneness with the rocks, with the trees, with animals, with flowers, with all energy forms. There is that Oneness that pervades all — no boundaries, no separation, perfect understanding.

This Divine Presence guides you, guards you, and protects you. There is nothing to resist It. It is Life itself, and Life is for you not against you. That Life Presence is in everything. It is beyond opinions, past the effect, appearance, or the negative. Spiritual truth responds to you and takes you through anything if you acknowledge It. You'll learn to talk with It, and you'll receive direct, intuitive answers. It does not choose for you, but continually brings you an inner awareness of answers so you can make the right choice.

Faith is the essence of this communion. You develop your trust and knowledge by testing and measuring this principle. "I know that I know." Even though you may not appear to be succeeding, as long as you know the Spiritual Truth, you get better and better with your practice of principle. You must recognize that with this Presence you are also dealing with an impersonal law. As long as you use it without coercion, manipulation, or scheming and your motivation and intent are to develop the best within you, only good is the result. It's a commitment. Once you commit yourself to the pathway of Truth, there's no turning back. There's nothing that will ever fulfill you again. Only Truth accomplishes this!

This divine law is your servant. The only discipline required is to use this law properly with love. You have all of the love you'll ever need within you. Love is an acceptance of Truth within, and you can use the results of this love you're experiencing without limit.

What you are working out is expanding and moving from personal love to impersonal love, which is perfect freedom. It is detachment, not indifference, from the mind, emotions, and body. Impersonal love acts as a witness or observer. When you can love that way, you have the healing power active in every experience. There is no need for you to fight the opinions of others or waste your time arguing over these laws. You stay centered and infused with the Higher Power within. Follow the inner light of your own consciousness — that's where Truth is. And you know the truth for any particular situation you are in. Use what you have. *Know you are always in your right place, in the right way in the now for your growth and unfoldment.*

Whatever you identify with, you become. With a deep feeling, identify with happiness, success, peace, love, security, all of these things, and you become them. You cannot be two things at the same time, and therefore, if you identify with financial prosperity, you lift yourself out of poverty; or if you identify with love, you draw love to you.

Whatever you resist, you give power to, and by giving it your attention, you bring it into reality. That which you fear comes upon you. What you resist you will actually attract, and become like, until such time as the reality of The Real You is established. Don't fight your fears and insecurities, look through them and identify with their opposites.

The laws of Spirit are natural laws. It is still a part of the whole universal structure of natural law, like the law of gravity, the law of reflection, the law of repetition. The only difference between the use of spiritual laws and the other natural laws is that most people have not realized that they can use spiritual law as consciously as they do other laws.

Everything around you is energy in form. Spiritual energy is at the center of everything. It is at the very center, the Power and Pattern, of everything you see — the rock, the tree, the bird, the bee. There is a spiritual integrity in everything, and if you acknowledge It within yourself, It responds to you in all its power in the natural flow of life.

Desires

The Spiritual Self reveals Itself to you as desire and intuition. Desire can be put under three labels — the false desire, impatient desire, and heart's desire. Any of these move you into action.

A **false desire** is painful, compulsive, nervous, frustrated, and angry. It keeps you running in a circle, but you don't know where you are going! False desires are those that make you hunt for the right place for you. If it's not in Phoenix, you move to Los Angeles thinking your answers are there. When you move, you take you and your false desires with you. False desire does not satisfy your hunger. The best thing to do is to stay in the situation you're in until you really complete the patterns of consciousness that have kept you where you are. Look around you, for what's around you is you, and let it show you where you are in thought and emotion. *Change your thinking, change your life.* If you have inner desires, they are guidelines to find your inner Self, and they are valid to you. You must express that which you desire on all levels. Sometimes you have to experience your lesser desires on your physical level to know that they're not good for you. Your code of ethics or code of integrity are your own codes. You know before anyone else can tell you that something is good or bad for you. So an outside system that's telling you what's good and bad is really only a guideline.

You must complete patterns. That's part of your spiritual integrity. Sometimes you have completed a pattern, but you've kept it in your consciousness and not released it. So you've got a worn-out condition and a completed situation that is not letting in the new patterns and your truth. It is important to let something go in consciousness to make room for the new experiences.

An **impatient desire** is like a credit card desire. It's like taking your credit card and spending right up to the hilt to get all the things that you want. You're spending before you really need that thing in your life. You are creating an unstable situation in consciousness. Impatient desires work with premature ideas. Everything in the universe comes under divine timing. There's a divine rhythm in your life. If you force, manipulate, scheme, or coerce, to satisfy a desire that is the same way you have to act to keep the same desire. Is it worth it?

Watch your impatient desires. Are you forcing a demonstration? Are you spending before you have it? If you are impatient, you will not succeed. You may have a beautiful idea for business, but the timing may be off, and therefore, it fails. Stop it. Relax. Take your time. Let your goal and idea have their own time of birthing, of coming into your reality under the law of growth. Be patient and trust, and you will succeed automatically.

Because of excessive use of credit cards, the feeling of having money is gone. How often do you touch and spend cash? If you have a feeling of lack, get all one dollar bills and go pay your electric bill. Develop the feeling of prosperity. If you feel you never have any money, carry some with you. Don't always write a check or use your credit card. Pay cash! That helps you redefine your prosperity consciousness.

You may see a pattern or rhythm in your life that tells you that you seem to create some sort of crisis before you produce. Become aware of what you are using as your motivation and intent to take you to your goal. Maybe you have to go through a ninety-day dry spell before you really have to produce. Check out your rhythm. You will see cycles of lack and cycles of prosperity. Don't ever get caught up with the outer world cycles of poverty and prosperity. For example, in real estate, realtors may predict a poor year because interest rates have gone up and no one is going to approve loans. That's not true. During the times of high interest rates, many people reached the highest peaks in sales because they didn't relate to the doom statistics or the law of averages. Divine Intelligence moved them in and through this period.

Everything is determined by the law of belief. What you believe to be true is true for you. When you deal with stocks, securities, investments, listen to your inner voice, not the outer world. You have to learn to work with and trust the inner intuitive force that will lead you to your heart's desires.

Your **heart's desires** are your greatest assets. They indicate the experiences you can have when you make your decisions to have them. You have to decide to have them and make room for them in your life. If you put them aside and push them down into your subconscious and you try to live up to other people's standards, you may really have to dig deeper into your subconscious to find your heart's desires again. Get quiet, listen to your heart, and find out what is real to you and what is not. Find that heart's desire or dream and crystallize it in your mind. Work with it until you produce it. That's what will take you to happiness, to that total fulfillment of your dreams. You can be a great success on the outer and still be lonely until you find your True Self. You can have a great family, home, and career and yet feel empty inside because you haven't done that thing that you came into life to do.

Heart's desires are a mighty potential awaiting your attention. They should never be ignored. With a deep spiritual understanding, they can now emerge in your life to fulfill your life. As you think about them, they stir within your consciousness as a baby stirs within the mother's womb. They want out. They want to be made visible by means of you. They are knocking on the door of your intuition, trusting that you will open the door. They also create motion, but their motion is a straight line to success. They don't move in a monotonous cycle. They flow. When there is no flow, quit all action until you clear your mind and clear your thinking. Then you continue.

Get out of monotonous routines and humdrum thinking. You are not living to seek approval or follow outside programming or preconceived ideas. Go with the feeling that you are in constant touch with Spirit, your Guiding Light.

To realize your desires, several times a day form an affirmation to direct the subconscious: "I accept all my desires and goals are divinely inspired and come to me from the Infinite Intelligence. I am guided, guarded, and protected in everything I do. I now accept and know that the spiritual center of my subconscious is now responding and that on which I stake my claim within is expressed right now in outer form."

There's a part of you that is centered and connected with this all-pervading Power. There is a part of you that is like the eye of the storm. You are calm when all around you is in uproar. Keep that center and you can handle anything. Stay in touch with It moment by moment. It's like you're two parts going through life — the Real You and the ego self. Keep the ego self under the control of the Higher Power, and you'll move through any situation in poise and grace.

You can examine any experience in your life, and you'll find the good that was behind the appearance, the potential that was stirred within you when you went through a particular trauma. See how it made you reach for courage and made you discover assets in yourself that you never knew you had. Every trauma brings forth more of the true greatness within, more trust in this Power. Your security is not in a person, place, or thing. Those things can be wiped out. People can leave you, and places can change. Your security is in your understanding of your spiritual integrity and your use of it, staying centered in It.

A Secret Life

If you're trying to lead a double life, you have a secret life and an open life. Remember, there are no secrets in the universe. Everyone uses the same subconscious mind; it is universal. If you are keeping a life in secret on the subconscious level, that's the Power level. When you do a treatment by staying silent, steady, and true to it, you use that knowledge in a constructive way. The subconscious mind produces whatever is energized within it. It's the same with a double life when you are lying to yourself. The secret life will be revealed because it is in the place where the law is acting to outpicture what is energized on the subconscious level. There are no secrets; eventually everything will be exposed, so be prepared to handle that secret life. Meet those awkward situations in your life as soon as you can. If you need to lie, know the consequences; be prepared to face the lie. If you think you need to cheat and steal to maintain prosperity, you will have to lie or steal to sustain it. And eventually you will have to pay the price for those actions! You are only as sick as your secrets.

Be honest with yourself. Take a look at your life and see where you are in denial of your truth. In the areas where you can't tell the truth because of fear, at least mentally know the truth and tell it to yourself. Don't lie to yourself! Know that the truth shall set you free. That's what it's all about. Deal with duality, or your two lives, until it finally comes into oneness. That's what you're seeking — oneness. This happens when the High Self is in control of the ego self. There's nothing to resist. Spirit, mind, and body flow continually ever reaching for the fourth dimension or cosmic consciousness or illumination into the greater life here and now on earth.

The ego self always demands feedback from the outside for approval. It demands approval to know that it exists. If your ego support is being pretty, you need to be keep being told you are pretty, or you don't feel pretty anymore. When you know you're beautiful because you are made in the image and likeness of God, you are living in the now, being the Real You. Neither praise or criticism matters because you're living in the now — being, becoming centered in joy, peace, calmness. You're comfortable with you and your world.

The ego state demands recognition. When you're in your true life work, you could care less about fame. In fact, you move more quietly and powerfully without it.

Pride has something to do with an outer set of values that society has set upon you, and if you feel you can't measure up to that set of values, you get depressed about it. Those values may be false and go against your natural truth. Choose integrity instead of pride or vanity. Integrity is your inner truth. Pride and vanity are ego opinions (mental).

Morals vs. Ethics

There is a difference between morals and ethics. For spiritual growth, replace morals with ethics. Morals are manners, rules, regulations, conventions, external patterns. They change frequently. Morals involve the proper conduct so your manners are acceptable in an era on a given day.

Ethics handle the forces of your nature so they function constructively in a permanent way in your life. Social systems' morals and manners change in every region. Ethics are laws of behavior based on spiritual truths that support individual creativity and freedom. To discover the spiritual core of a social order, a firm ethical foundation is needed. Then order can be built on a solid foundation — order, based on knowledge of your spiritual nature, not on prejudices or ignorance. In such a world, everyone's future is fulfilled — with joy, not pain. Morals are man-made and ethics are of God.

The ego state, seeking approval and status, usually carries you to excess, and your pleasure becomes your pain. It can become compulsive — *more creates more*. Maybe you liked a little alcohol to help you socialize, and now you're addicted to it; or the doctor prescribed an antidepressant for you to deal with stress created by competitiveness, and now you can't function without it; or you tried drugs just to experiment, to be more at ease in groups, and now you're addicted. Morals put pressures on a person to live up to a false set of values and set up feelings of failure if the morals are disobeyed.

The inner Self knows. It moves you in a natural flow of life. There's no resistance by you. You move in an orderly balanced, rhythmic fashion. You're comfortable with you and you know that you know, no matter what the world is saying. You live by inner principles of Life, common to all of Life. These principles work for you anywhere in the world.

Age

Age can be a factor in how you view the world. You may be intimidated by age until you realize there is no age in mind. Age is the chronological measure of time in the outer. Age, looked at from the inner Self represents an attitude, and so clear thinking, joy, happiness, vitality, and centeredness have no age limitations. In Spirit, there's no such thing as age or loneliness. There's no reason for you to grow old and lonely. If your attitude is young, you'll always have people around you, things to do, and you're being and becoming until the last minute. If you really develop yourself, you'll be able to gracefully move to the next dimensions without stopping. You just shed the body, and go on. The underlying fear of death and the underlying fear of pain is intimidation, and much of your behavior is determined by these old patterns and attitudes. Everything in life tells us there is no beginning and no end — there is simply here and now. Is birth a beginning or an end? Is death an end or a new beginning?

There are no two persons alike in this universe, and for this reason, there must be a unique place for you in the plan of life. There is a Divine Pattern to the universe which you observe all about you. This Divine Pattern would be imperfect without you. Dare to be yourself. Accept all the good there is. Whatever you desire, believe that you have it now. Say, "I release all fear, all doubt. I am secure in Spirit. I know what is mine claims me, knows me, flows through me as me. I accept the gift of life now."

Once you have recognized that there is a Divine Presence, which is your guiding star of assurance and certainty, then you become equally certain and recognize the Universal Law of Mind as your servant. The law of mind is the natural principal you use. Your faith in this law of mind causes It to act upon your faith, to bring into your experience those things you accept. Never use the law of mind for destructive purposes. What you give out to the world comes back to you like a boomerang. When you use this law of mind with love, you can use it without any sense of limitation or fear.

There is a creative center within your subconscious mind which is all-wise and knows the answers to all questions. Remember, the subconscious does not argue or talk back to you. When you give your subconscious mind a chance to perform, it is important to let go and let it do its work. Too many times you set up impediments and delays by your conscious mind, and when this is done, you are denying the wisdom and intelligence which are in your subconscious mind. You give your subconscious mind a problem to solve, and then tell it that it cannot solve the problem. It is like you start a fire and then put it out in the same breath. This you do many times by saying you have to, but you cannot, or you want to, but cannot. This type of programming of your subconscious mind leads to mental and emotional congestion followed by sickness and neurosis.

Start your day off with a morning exercise and say to yourself, "I am great. I am wonderful. I am a success right now. I am beautiful. I am perfect health." Then use your meditations, your blessings, and your treatments to control the energy in your relationship to the world outside.

Sensitivity

Personal sensitivity falls under three categories: sympathy, empathy, and compassion.

Sympathy is the ego state. It looks at a situation and says, "Oh, isn't that awful? Look what they're going through." What you're really saying is "Thank God it isn't me." There is no real involvement or even caring.

Compassion without wisdom is martyrdom. "Look what I did for my children, and look how they treat me." If you give too much and take care of others needs before yourself, you are keeping everything out of balance. Remember, you make the choice to over-give. This is definitely about caring, but goes beyond a healthy balance. Your energy goes out too far and leaves you depleted and helpless.

Empathy is compassion with wisdom, understanding, and love. Empathy is understanding the basic nature of the human being. Since everyone uses the same Divine Intelligence on the spiritual level, there is only One, and you are better able to understand the basic needs of a person. You can honestly and lovingly say it like it is. If you can help, you can say *yes*; if you can't help, you can say *no*. If you get into someone else's space and you don't belong there, you're not doing them any service. Empathy is the wisdom and the courage to say, "This is what I can do. This is what I won't do," rather than automatic sharing of another's feelings or experiences.

Sensitivity is also knowing your world through the five senses — sight, hearing, taste, smell, and touch. Generally speaking, this is how you know where you are on your journey. Your use of the five senses expands from the inner plane as you reveal more of your true spiritual nature and as you express more spiritual integrity.

Sight. One takes in knowledge by image much faster that any other way. Inner sight expands that knowledge so that you see the truth behind the appearance or the fact. You see beauty beyond ugliness, health beyond sickness. You see the natural order of balance, rhythm, and harmony in everything that surrounds you. You see beyond death's door to life ever unfolding, eternal, and limitless.

Hearing. You keep your ear tuned to the Universal Intelligence, to the truth that sets you free. You hear beyond the negative complaining masses. You hear the song of the universe. You hear the grass grow, the coming of spring, the blossoms opening, the leaves falling, the stealth of cold winter, and the song of the night bird.

Taste. Experience texture in new dimensions, pleasures beyond measure as you enjoy the fruits and food of your labor. Your taste warns you, guards you, and therefore, protects your body. You know what is good for your well-being.

Smell. This sense reveals secrets beyond measure, greater pleasures from your surroundings, greater appreciation of all of nature; freshness of spring, the good earth, of a forest fire or rain or the ocean. A greater awareness of where you are right now — an extension of your other senses.

Touch. Perhaps the greatest of the senses is touch. Yours can be an energizing healing touch. The magnetic healing energy, the love energy, flows through every part of your being and is a blessing to those who come in contact with you. Your touch can be with your hands, your eyes, your voice. Yours can be a touch of encouragement, well-wishing, love, your touch speaks louder than your voice expressing words of love, caring, being, recognition. Your touch breaks down the barriers of rejection, hate, low self-esteem, non-acceptance. You can develop the ability of touch through stroking and caring for animals. They never reject love. They respond and are the most forgiving, unless they are specifically otherwise programmed.

Yes, you want your vision to develop in truth and you want to see beyond the negative. You want to see beauty beyond ugliness, love beyond hate, to experience the joy of moving from ignorance to enlightenment. You want to be able to hear the sound of the universe and relate to it and enjoy it — the inaudible sound. You want to hear beyond the complaining, beyond the pressures of can'ts and musts to peace, to calmness, to truth, to poetry, to music. You want to be able to taste and enjoy texture. You want to be able to touch and use that as a healing touch to express love and the truth so you can give energy, so you can give everyone who comes in contact with you back to themselves. Your hugs are energy hugs. You have it to give because you are in tune with Spirit, with Pure Energy. You want to be sensitive to good everywhere and to the outpicturing of that divine inheritance that is yours right now.

Energy Discernment

As you develop your spiritual integrity, you are also developing a deeper sensitivity to the truth of yourself, the truth of the universe, and how you function. This is the sixth sense, this is intuition.

Intuition vs. Psychic

Spirit speaks to you through intuition. You block the spiritual integrity of your being when you are tense or emotionally, physically, and mentally uptight. Relax into peace and poise, into Spirit and into the proper tension for the task at hand to keep the flow of your life open to your direct knowing or intuition.

Intuition goes beyond the five senses. The word intuition means inner teaching. It's an inner knowingness that comes

– Figure 16 –

ENERGY DISCERNMENT: INTUITION VS. PSYCHIC

INTUITION	PSYCHIC
Cause	Effect
Spiritual level — The Real You Oneness (neutral)	Mental level — emotional, ego Duality (positive/negative)
Now	Past — future
Action from within	Action from without
Sixth sense	Five senses
Divine Mind	Race mind — (the human group consciousness)
Superconscious	Subconscious programming — ego
Action	Reaction
Peaceful — relaxed	Trauma, trance
Truth	Fragmented knowledge
Flow — orderly sequence	Stumbling blocks
Feeling	Emotions, questions, doubts
Trusting	Forced plan of action, negative or positive
Spontaneous	Impulsiveness

from your Spiritual Source. It's an awareness that goes beyond logic and understanding or language; it operates from feeling. It's that hunch or a keen, quick insight without direct reasoning. When your sixth sense beckons you to pay attention, listen because that's your guidance for right decisions. True intuition is not involved with getting — it deals with self-awareness. It reveals what you have always been. It is appropriate for the situation. It always takes you to a greater good.

When you are receiving intuitive knowledge, it is not from the psychic plane. It's direct knowledge from within. There is a definite difference between the psychic and intuition (Figure 16). *Two things cannot occupy the same space at the same time.* This means if you are in the spiritual realm, you cannot be on the psychic plane (ego) at the same time. They are two different places!

It can be destructive to look to the psychic plane for guidance, as it is the plane of many minds and not of the One Mind. Psychic knowledge comes through the five senses, from the outside in. Intuition comes from within and is the truth for you at that moment. Be open to your intuition and let the psychic and the development of the five senses come under the control of your sixth sense or spiritual integrity and conscious choice. Never let the psychic energy decide for you or take control of you.

Despite common belief, psychic phenomenon is a natural process, but it is outside science or natural knowledge. You have the ability to use your intuition in a deepened extrasensory way as you develop your Spiritual Self. The psychic information is from the ego state of the mental and emotional levels (your personality). Precognition, clairaudience, clairvoyance, clairsenscion, and telepathy are a deeper use of the five senses that are reading duality, race-mind.

In channeling, you allow some psychic personality to take over your body, and your individual self is set aside. Many times in channeling, when an entity or psychic soul is speaking through you, you do not know what is being said or going on; your ego has been set aside, and you have lost your ability to choose under these conditions. For the period of time that you are channeling, you do not exist. Your purpose for being here on earth is to be you, to grow, to unfold, to be a unique expression of the Creative Life Force. If anyone or anything is coming through you, you are to be in control. Your gift of life is choice, so it is important never to give that gift away!

Intuition comes from the spiritual level. Intuition leads you into growth. The psychic leads you into the past and into the future. Intuition leads you into right action now. It's easy to get caught up in phenomena of reading the past and the future rather than growth and understanding in the now. The spiritual level functions at its optimum only when you are relaxed into proper tension. You can experience an emotional trauma or go into a trance when you have a psychic experience. Most mentally insane people are being bombarded by psychic experience. They have lost control of the conscious mind. If you get caught up in psychic energy, it can break down your conscious choices because you're allowing an outside control to take over subconsciously. Your life work can be getting back control of these outside forces. The subconscious level is where the power is.

If you're picking up psychic messages, you are picking up from the ego, which is stuck in the preprogrammed, preconceived, and the outside condition or intellectual or emotional growth at this point. This information is both negative and positive, it is duality. Reading someone else's mind is not necessarily good. You don't need to know what's going on in someone else's head any more than you have to read their mail. It is dangerous to assume this information is factual or the truth.

In a psychic reading, the psychic reads fragmented information that is both positive and negative. For example, Aunt Sadie was prone to give you lots of advice on this side of the world. It wasn't very good, but it was offered freely. One day Aunt Sadie crosses over to a cosmic address, and she contacts you psychically and gives you a tip on real estate. You love her so you let her in. Her advice is no better from there than it was here. Just because Aunt Sadie's coming from a different dimension doesn't mean the advice is any better, it's still Aunt Sadie.

A psychic reading is the ability to function and express what is on the subconscious level. A psychic has to come through personality patterns stored in the subconscious. Already, the information is fragmented. Then the psychic comes into your space because you have given permission to enter your aura. Both of you have opened up subconscious personality to subconscious personality, and the information becomes contaminated. If the psychic is feeling ill, you can pick up the negative patterns and bring them right into your own consciousness. If you're being confused and upset and you can't decide with your own information, then you begin to decide on the psychic's terms. You are avoiding the responsibility of making your own decisions. There is no time on the subconscious level, so a psychic can read only the thoughts and emotional patterns that are energized in your aura at the specific point of time of the session. What you're thinking now on the conscious and subconscious level, when it is energized, creates your future. But if you change your mind, the reading will change, and therefore, your future changes. The future is not your place in time. Now is all you have!

A psychic may read you and tell you that you are going to have an accident. If you're not exercising spiritual control, the psychic can help you create that accident because the subconscious says yes to everything. You accept it very innocently and start producing the circumstances to have that accident. What you picture and what you expect are what you get. If the psychic says the accident will occur in two weeks, you know that information is invalid because there's no time in the subconscious. The psychic's information is only relevant for that one split second that you're in the reading session. It has nothing to do with your tomorrow unless you've accepted this information as your truth, at which time you've given full control of your life to a psychic. And you are not meeting your responsibility as a spiritual person.

If you stay relaxed into the Truth of you and use your intuition, you get information in the here and now that is pertinent to action in the here and now. The psychic gets information that is from the past and future, and that is avoiding the here and now. Your true space in time on earth is in the here and now.

When the psychic tells you something about the future, it's a premature idea or an impatient desire. You need to keep your mind free, in the here and now, in touch with Spirit, and It will give you the higher message that will take you intuitively into right action.

People are communicating in the silence all the time. If you are communicating to another spiritually, it is an infusion of Truth, and it is Oneness. There's no separation. The spiritual level is beyond language — it's pure love, it's pure energy, it's pure wisdom — there is only One.

Sometimes you can experience a space where words would destroy the beauty that embraces you. It's silent, but it's a strong communication with ultimate Good. It's a feeling of oneness where you are unifying with pure love in a situation. There is no resistance in this experience — only harmony, order, balance, and perfect timing. It is total and beautiful communication without space and time or verbalizing.

Nightly Review

Before you go to bed at night, do this nightly review. It prevents forming new inhibitions and repressions and ensures a good sleep. The subconscious mind takes over while the conscious mind sleeps. It continues to work on the thoughts and feelings that the conscious mind ended with at day's end. It is important, then, to review and redirect the subconscious mind to work on a constructive, productive thought and feeling. So before you go to sleep, affirm, "I sleep in peace and wake in joy."

In the evening, here is an exercise to help you see how well you've done and where you need to improve. Write down the five levels — physical, emotional, mental, social, and spiritual (Figure 17). Put down two columns, false and true. Under physical, ask yourself the following questions: Did I do anything compulsive today? Did I have a cold? Did I have a headache? Was I tense? Anxious? Very, very tired? For the True Self, if you came through the day physically as you should, you feel full of good health expressing or experiencing vitality or the proper

– Figure 17 –

NIGHTLY REVIEW

LEVELS	FALSE	TRUE
Physical	Anything compulsive — colds, headaches, tension, restlessness.	Health, vitality, energetic.
Emotional	Overexcited, depressed, resentful, anxious, hostile, seeking to please, critical, judging, denial, condemning, lack, fear, anger.	Calm, serene, givingness, forgivingness, patience, perseverence, sensitive to good.
Mental	Negative thoughts, habits of thinking destructively, I can't; I have to; I don't have; etc. It's impossible; It won't work; If only; Yes, but; I wish.	Constructive, productive, imaging what you want to experience. Knowing everything is possible. Keeping your mind focused in the now.
Spiritual	Unawareness, indecisiveness, lonely, separated from your good, isolation.	Order, harmony, balance, calm, relaxed, vital, feel dynamic, alert, listening attitude, secure. At home wherever you are in the universe.
Social	Antagonism in relationships, suspicion, mistrust, hate, jealousy, envy, fear, rejection, avoidance, denial.	Harmony, each relationship makes you feel more of your True Self, growth.

At the end of your day, ask yourself these questions:

How did I use my time today?
Was my focus in the past, present or future?

Did I exercise the body?

Did I just intellectualize today, or did I listen
and receive guidance from my inner self?

In my relationship with people, did I identify with negativity and illness,
lack and limitation, or did I recognize the Divine harmony
and stay focused on what is right?

tension for the task at hand — a feeling of energy with the proper tiredness for what you went through, not total fatigue.

For the emotional level, the questions are: Was I overexcited? Was I depressed? Was I resentful? Anxious? Hostile? Did I speak to please? Was I critical? Judging? Self-condemning? If you came through properly in integrity, you came through the day calmly, serene, with givingness, forgiveness, patience, with Spirit, and sensitive to only good. You're centered and in balance.

For the mental level, ask the following questions: Was I negative today in my thoughts or the use of words? Did I return to habits of destructive thinking? Did I use words like I can't; I have to; It won't work; It's impossible; If only; Yes, but; I wish; I hope. (Hope is a weak fear.) Or was I constructive and productive? Did I image what I want to experience? Did I keep centered and stay on the path? Was I coordinating and cooperating with my goal? Was my attitude one of optimism, knowing that everything is possible? Did I stop and unify with Spirit wherever I felt uncomfortable? Did I keep my mind focused on the now?

On the spiritual level, did I experience loneliness, indecisiveness, or feel separated from my good? Loneliness is a denial of Spirit. Pray without ceasing means being linked into Spirit, moment by moment, knowing that Presence and Power is always there. Did I come through the day in order, harmony, balance, relaxed, calm, and vital, feeling dynamic and alert? Did I stay in a listening attitude? Secure? Do I feel at home wherever I am in the universe?

On the social level, was I antagonistic in my relationships? Did I feel suspicion, mistrustful, hate, jealousy, envy, anger, fear? Did I feel harmonious in my relationships? Did I feel that with everyone who came into my life today I gave them back to themselves? Did I stay centered and true to myself for my growth in relationships?

How do you measure up for the day? Were you too social, too physical, too mental? Ask yourself what you can to do to return to balance.

A Checklist for Keeping Centered

- Are you functioning in the here and now? Are you comparing, competing, self-condemning? Know that you are always in your right place, in the right way, in the right now for the level of your understanding and acceptance of good. Bless the good and grow with it. You are moving from ignorance to enlightenment.

- Are you in your own space, or are you assuming for others? Perhaps your discomfort or imbalance is the result of preprogramming, preconceived ideas, pre-thinking, jumping to conclusions, or seeking approval. Get back into your own space. Give up attitudes, opinions, judgements, and criticism of anyone, anything.

- Do you feel you're going to lose something by being honest — that you may lose a friend or lose some good by saying it like it is? That is not true. Being real is being loving. Being honest is the kindest thing you can do to establish integrity in any situation. That which belongs to you stays with you by right of consciousness, you only have to accept it.

- Do you feel that emptiness is bad, that when you are lonely or desolate you have been abandoned? Are you looking at the half-empty or the half-full glass? The law of vacuum applies here. When something moves out of your life, some greater good moves in. Look at the spaces as a blessing and look at the vacuum as being filled by greater good; then stake your claim on it. Change is life, life is change. If you're complacent and stagnating and trying to play it safe, you are on the periphery of life and not living in the mainstream of it. You are never alone or abandoned. Spirit is always in you! All the love, all the healing power, all the prosperity are right where you are.

- Are you seeking approval? If you whittle yourself down to please everybody, you only wind up a pile of shavings.

- Are you spiritually centered? Do you feel that the Power and Presence is ever-available?

- Are you so heavenly inclined that you are no earthly good? Are you trying to be holy? Are you trying to stay in meditation so you can escape life? Keep in mind that life is Spirit, mind, and body in action, ebb and flow.
- What level are you functioning on now? If you're having a problem on the emotional level, you have four other levels where it can be worked on and solved. Work it out on the physical, mental, or social level, or go directly to Spirit and dissolve your problem. Accept solutions and answers. Rather than staying on the same level as the problem, it is easier to go to a different level so you can break loose from the pattern. Sometimes it is helpful to go to the social level and release to a friend who just listens or to go to a spiritual mind practitioner, someone who is detached, to help you through. Go to a person who has the courage to monitor you and tell you what he or she is seeing and hearing from your space and remind you of the spiritual laws that apply to this situation. This is a person who does not make you feel blame, shame, or guilt.
- Are you concentrating on cause (inner) or effect (outer)? You established cause by choice of thoughts and words. What are you identifying with now? In what direction are you focusing your mind? Are you going to Spirit? Are you going to the psychic? Are you going to friends? Are you living on the mental, emotional, and physical levels only? Cause is always invisible. Effect is always the outer result. If you have established a choice that makes you uncomfortable, go back and change the thought behind it. Affirm what you desire — divine order, balance, timing, harmony. Use the spiritual laws and work with the truth of Spirit, and you'll correct the pattern and get back on track. The outpicturing result of what you think is effect. What is around you is you. If you need to ask the questions, "Where am I and who am I?" look where you are. Who's in your presence? Listen to the talk around you. What are you hearing? Life around you is your mirror!
- You are always order, balance, rhythm, harmony. You are always Power and Presence, wisdom, peace, love, poise,

prosperity. Your denial of it doesn't chase it away. It is your birthright to experience joy!

- Stop associating change with loss. Change gets you out of your ruts. Nothing is ever lost, it is only misplaced.
- Know within yourself that right action is taking place in your life right now. That Teacher within you is leading you to the right place, into the right way, into the right now for the level of your growth. You are great. You are wonderful. You have everything to be and become. Accept it!
- The ultimate goal of the Divine in you, as you, is cosmic consciousness here on earth. Each individual has the opportunity to reveal the truth, and that truth comes from one consistent source. The closer you relate to that Inner Truth, the healthier, happier, more joyful, prosperous, and creative you are.
- So what can you expect from this Divine Intelligence? It does not know equal, fair, or just — It only knows consciousness. Life gives you what you accept subconsciously. It does not give you what you deserve, need, or want.

True knowing is when you have said yes to your divine inheritance. You experience unity consciousness — oneness, harmony, peace, joy, wholeness, prosperity. You live by Law and Love, principles, not personality. You are proactive, not reactive. You are detached, but not indifferent. You are discerning, not judgmental. You are comfortable with change, and you move beyond "I believe" to "I know." It works! The Real You is your reality!

2

Being the Real You

Chapter Twelve

The Real You in Relationships

After you have achieved a deep understanding of who you are and where you are, it is time to move your attention from self to outer relationships. What is around you is your mirror reflection of your subconscious. Knowing this, it is easier to discern the energies around you and make changes necessary within yourself to flow more harmoniously throughout your earth life. Keep in mind, you are only seeking to change yourself and your consciousness so the world around you reflects your peace and harmony.

In doing so, it is helpful to understand the state of your own consciousness. It works really well if you divide the programming (from the outer) of your personality or ego state (Figure 18) into these areas: the parent, the child, the adult. These tools are from the work of Dr. Eric Berne in his book, *Games People Play*. This facilitates developing techniques in communication skills.

– Figure 18 –

HEALTHY DIVISION OF ADULT, CHILD AND PARENT

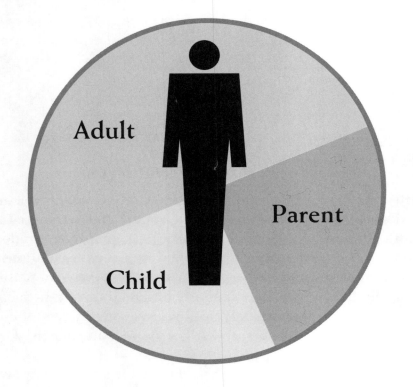

How To Tell What State You Are In

One of the ways to determine whether you or someone around you is coming from the parent, adult, or child perspective, is by statements that are made. Clues to these various states are certain words that are used, and quite often indicate the ego state. The physical characteristics of our body movements give us clues. Inflection of voice and emotional responses give us clues. Here are some examples of these clues to help determine various ego states:

1. Parent word clues: "You should clean up your plate. Go ahead and eat it. It will keep up your energy." "How many times have I told you … I'm going to put a stop to this once and for all. If I were you … "

Parent physical clues: Pointing of index finger; hands on hips; wringing hands; folded arms; patting on head.

2. Adult word clues: "Why, What, When, How, Where, Who, I think, "It is my opinion," or "That piece of cake must have at least 400 calories. I think I'll skip it."

Adult physical clues: Hands and body relaxed and at ease; head straight forward, not tilted to one side.

3. Child world clues: "I wish, I want, I don't care, Good, better, best, I'll get him, I'm happy, I'm hurt, What a yummy cake. I could eat the whole thing."

Child physical clues: Tears, laughter, shrugging shoulders, raising hand for permission to speak.

The Parent

What is called the *parent* programming is anything you have learned from the past that has created your value systems — all of the *should's, ought to's, and musts.* Much of this programming comes from your parents, culture, school training, and religion. Much of it is not the way you *really* want to be, but you perform from this traditional behavior because it is all you know about yourself. The parent part of you is taught by your outer experiences.

By staying detached and watching your communications, you can quickly see when you are parenting yourself or others. All parent energies create a defensive or compliant attitude in the one to whom the communication is directed. Based on that awareness, speaking from the parent is not an effective way of creating harmony in any relationship. In many cases, it is a put-down. The person has a resistance to you and often rebels at the message. Therefore, the message is not communicated very well and misunderstood at best.

The Child

The *child* set of patterns in your consciousness is comprised of all the past emotions and feelings, positive or negative, that are aroused. Just as you would not allow a child to control your life lessons, even now you do not want the child, or the emotions, running your consciousness. Emotional child reactions create victims.

The typical response to a parent communication is a response from the child that is an emotional reaction. The reaction is in defense to an aggressive parent energy. Therefore, there really is no communication because no one is listening. The parent is busy telling and the child is defending its position by reacting emotionally. Nothing is accomplished.

Many times in the child state are stored the "I am not okay" feelings. These are feelings that "everyone in the world is 'okay' but me." When the emotional child dominates the ego state, it creates a dysfunctional adult. That is, someone who does not complete tasks or finish projects. It creates a poorly performing adult who lacks drive or consistency in any situation, an adult who cannot be depended on to perform. Often times this type is socially and sexually inhibited.

The Adult

The part of your consciousness that comes to the rescue is the *adult* state, and it deals directly with the now. It updates the parent tapes from the past and makes them relevant to the present, and it quiets the emotional child.

The adult part of you is a thought process. This part of your consciousness must always be in charge or standing guard at the doorway of your mind to control the child state responses and update the information from the past (the parent) so you can make valid decisions regarding your own growth and unfoldment. It also ensures that the Real You is expressing your own spiritual insights.

The "adult" makes decisions from three sources of information: the parent; the child; and the data that the adult has stored and continues to gather. The adult makes logical and rational decisions. Once you have established when the parent, the child, or the adult is operating in your consciousness, you can observe when those same energies are reflecting back to you in a relationship. This helps you to determine if your communication is going to be effective or not — keeping in mind the parent tapes of should's, ought to's, and musts that trigger the child (an emotion in the conversation) or trigger the same parent energy back to you. To be heard, the adult has to be present to sum up the responses to make the message current or relevant in the now. Most importantly, in order that the communication is heard clearly, it must come from the adult and be delivered to an adult.

Even though we love the child in us, there is a time when the child's behavior becomes intolerable or unacceptable, and the adult must rescue the message.

Parent-Child Marriages

Many marriages consist of a parent/child relationship. One establishes the power structure as parent and makes all the decisions on all major issues. The other carries the child, or the emotional load, and makes all the emotional responses for the marriage. This doesn't work for long because you are a whole individual, and when a part of you is not expressing, it is being suppressed causing resentment and hostility. Communication fails. It creates a fear-based, approval-seeking situation.

Traditional relationships are often the half-and-half syndrome, where two halves make a whole. Never are you a half of anything! You are a totally self-contained unit of the creative life force. A healthy marriage or relationship creates space for two individuals to harmonize their pathways. This creates support, encouragement, inspiration, motivation for each one to be the best they can be, to become self-actualized, and self-reliant. There is no bonding of two people becoming one. Give up your bonding, blending, and blaming, shaming, and guilt. None of these works in a relationship.

Maleness and Femaleness — Wholeness

Keep in mind that you function spiritually, mentally, emotionally, physically, and socially. The energy used on the mental level is positive in polarity. Here is where you decide or choose the forms or structures in your life. This energy is assertive, creative, brings about change, is protective, active, and dynamically builds the structure or the nest. It is usually represented by the right side of the body. In the Eastern philosophies, it is called the yang energy and is traditionally masculine.

The energy used on the feeling (emotional) level is traditionally the feminine energy and is negative in polarity. It functions as intuition, your spiritual connection. It creates an environment of harmony. It deals with home, passive-conservative earth energies. It is the nesting quality of you. Generally, it is represented by the left side of the body. In Eastern philosophies, it is known as the yin energy. It is the mother, the nurturing energy.

To become a healthy, harmonious individual, the balance between the masculine (mental) and the feminine (feeling, intuitive) must both take place within you, whether you are physically male or female. It is often said that the healthy marriage takes place within you, when this balance is achieved and expresses easily through you as you. Since the law of attraction brings to you your equivalent, you, as a whole person, draw to you another whole person. Two whole people then participate in a healthy relationship. The positive polarity (mental, masculine) and the negative polarity (feeling, feminine) balance each other, and you now become a neutral, balanced, whole person attracting to you complete patterns of growth. You now have the Divine Intelligence flowing through you because there is no resistance or stress involved in anything you do. You can still enjoy your child and become a parent when necessary. The spiritual self, the Real You in charge, the adult, is always observing and knows when to step in to keep a healthy balance. It is all focus and flow!

Chapter Thirteen

Assertiveness

As a person, there are certain human rights that help you stay in charge of energy and stay on a pathway of honesty. All of these rights are based on your motivation and intent to be the best and most honest person you can be telling the truth about where you are right now in what you see, feel, and hear.

Your Rights as a Person

- You have a right to do anything as long as your intent and motivation are not to hurt someone or take away from another person, and you are telling your truth.
- To maintain your integrity, you have the right to express your feelings as long as you take responsibility for what you say and you use an "I" message (the adult) rather than an accusing "you" message (the parent), even if someone feels hurt by the message. Feeling hurt is their choice, not yours.
- It is your right not to explain or give reasons for justifying your own behavior.
- You can also change your mind at any time. It is so important to practice this right because often you have new facts or insights, and to be true to yourself and to be honest, it may require a change of mind. You no longer need to ask for permission or obey anyone else's wishes or seek approval.
- You have the right to be illogical in making decisions. When you live by intuitive insights, you don't know why it is right, but deep down inside of you, you know that you know.

- You have the right not to care. That does not mean avoidance or denial. It means you have given all the love and knowledge you can in the situation, and it no longer is a priority to you. You have completed all the actions you can, and you have learned the lessons and are finished with the situation. It is time to move on!
- You have a right to make mistakes. There is no shame, blame, or guilt. There is only right action. You learn, grow, and go on improving your life as you take responsibility for what happens to you.
- If you accept the responsibility for helping another person in problem solving, you also have the right to discern or speak your thoughts in the situation.
- At any time, you have the right to remove yourself from a negative situation. Speak up and say, "You have told me all the things that are wrong. Now tell me what is right in this situation." If you do not say no to negativity, you are saying yes to it, and more negativity is attracted to you. Change the flow of energy to focus on the answer, not the problem.

These laws, these human rights, are the basics for assertive behavior. Your purpose of life, your birthright, is to be the Real You, without changing your behavior to seek someone's approval. If you are wondering when these rights are to be exercised, ask yourself these questions:

- How important is this situation to me?
- How will I feel afterwards if I don't express what I feel or think in this situation?
- Is it appropriate for me to assert myself in this situation? In other words, am I being dishonest by not telling how I feel and think?

The reasons assertiveness works is because it is a positive way of communication rather than one of manipulation, submission, or hostility. When people know where you are coming from, they have more trust in understanding themselves and their relationship to you. This leads to a more satisfying and enriched personal relationship with people because they have an opportunity to make a more honest response. Everyone is entitled to express honest thoughts, feelings and beliefs.

Evaluating Communications

To be successful in the use of communication skills, the spiritually guided inner adult is the one who must be in charge. To evaluate the different behaviors, you can use the following definitions of each type.

Assertive Behavior — The Adult State

To be assertive, your motivation or intent is to express thoughts and feelings, act on your rights and feel good about yourself (the adult). Also to be truthful and honest in communication to advance a concept of clarity. Your attitude is open, honest, caring, communicative, gentle, and trusting. You listen to feedback from others and remain non-defensive. The result of this stance is the attitudes of the person responding are open and cooperative and show appreciation for the communication. This person is likely to respond with self-confidence and demonstrate good self-esteem because of your honesty.

Non-Assertive Behavior — The Parent-Child State

The motivation and intent of non-assertive behavior are to avoid conflict and to seek approval. Operating in this mode, you want to avoid hurting feelings or offending anyone. You keep peace by putting another's rights above your own. The attitude of the non-assertive is indirect, fearful, and defensive. You are eager to keep peace at any price. On the surface, this may seem altruistic because you put others' needs first before your own needs are met. This is dishonest, and creates imbalance — and eventually resentment. The attitude of the person responding is closed, not open. There is an underlying feeling of irritation and annoyance because subconsciously you know when someone is not level-ing with you. Sometimes the responding person acts superior to the communication, and the communication is filled with frus-tration and indecision.

Aggressive Behavior — Critical, Heavy Parent Ego State

The motivation and intent of the aggressive personality is to be right at any cost. The purpose is to dominate, intimidate, label, or put down. The attitude is open, but disrespectful of others' rights and is often explosive. Actions are judgmental and punishing and are frequently defensive. However, an individual may feel guilt (child) after displaying this kind of behavior.

The attitude of the person responding to this aggressive energy may be fear of the communication, he may then give in to pressure. They will automatically feel defensive and resentful, feel put down, punished, and taken advantage of. This attitude creates a negative self-image. The followers of the aggressive personality rarely disagree and very seldom tell the truth. They act like the children of a heavy parent. There is no real commu-nication between the two parties.

Passive-Aggressive Behavior — Child, Parent, Ego State

The motivation and intent of this personality is to gain an aggressive end without being held responsible for the aggres-sion. They use guilt-inducing tactics to manipulate others. They use others to carry out their aggressive ends. For example, a third person is used to deliver a message. Instead of being direct, someone uses a best friend to say mean things about the third party, knowing the message will be delivered by the friend. The attitudes of the passive-aggressive are cowardly, fearful, and indirect. They are vengeful, punishing, and guilt-enduring. The attitude of the person responding to this behavior is often confusion. There is anger at the double message that is being given and a feeling of helplessness because there is not a clear direction for further communication. This type of personality is basically a troublemaker and very deceitful.

The Manipulation Traps

Generally, a manipulative act is not easily recognized because the habit is so ingrained that you do not realize you are doing it. It is conditioning that has gone on since childhood and now has become automatic. This, however, does not give you the right to take advantage of or manipulate another human being, and no one is going to put a stop to it but you. You are responsible for positive change in your life, and once you change one behavior, you change a whole series of related behaviors.

Following are some of the ways you can recognize this behavior (the child) and then make the appropriate adjustment.

Guilt. This emotion is instigated to control or to hurt you, often by a person in close relationships like family, marriages, or significant others. This is not worthy of your consideration. Leave the problem with the source and go on. It is their problem; do not make it yours.

Anger. This creates an uncomfortable circumstance and can be particularly unsettling to anyone who is unnerved by openly aggressive behavior. The key here is to remain perfectly calm and continue to respond in your adult with an "I" message, no matter how loudly your aggressor screams.

Criticism. Your adversary starts a general discussion and then in the middle of it switches to negative personal remarks about your behavior. The intention is to throw you off mental balance, get you frustrated and angry (which makes you a victim), and then switch back to the original discussion to get you to submit to the manipulation which was designed to control you in the first place.

Obligation. This is an unspoken and unsigned agreement. "If I do this for him, I know he will do this for me," — an assumption that is not always agreed upon.

Insecurity. The manipulation techniques used here are unsavory remarks, negative accusations, put-downs, or anything

that attacks your self-worth until you are confused and feel insecure about yourself in general.

Helplessness. This is a situation in which those close to you
claim that you are the only one who can help. You are the only
one that understands, and it is up to you to save them.

Teasing. By all appearances, this is supposed to be loving and
affectionate. However, the teaser has a hidden agenda and is
really making a statement of criticism underneath it all. This is a
definite ploy of manipulation and put-down.

Questions. This technique automatically puts you on the
defensive, especially when the person already knows the
answer and has set you up to trap you in a lie.

When you stay detached or in the observer position in consciousness, you can readily see and know when you are expressing in one of the above type energy modes. To be an effective,
loving, progressive, honest, harmonious, and truthful individual,
all of your communications must come from the Real You, your
spiritual identity. Then you come from the highest and best
within you and everyone benefits from your forthrightness and
integrity, which results in the best performance of life for all
involved. The spiritual energy inspires, motivates, uplifts,
encourages the best that you can be. It produces self-acceptance
and high self-esteem. It promotes self-reliance, self-actualization.
The spiritual energy is neutral, not dominating or intimidating. It
is ultimate freedom for all to express and to be. This is what you
desire to bring to a relationship, to develop enriching intimacy
and growth without risk or fears or loss of identity.

Verbal Responses to Manipulation

There are certain behavior responses to manipulation that enforce
your rights. Basically, you remain in your adult — calm, cool,
speaking firmly and authoritatively without becoming aggressive
or emotional, especially using anger. Reacting in anger in this kind
of situation only makes you a victim of the manipulation. Sarcasm
does not work either. It provokes more sarcasm, criticism, and
aggressive behavior from the adversary.

Following are some response methods.

Repeat technique. Establish the bottom line to the issue at hand and repeat your desires persistently, calmly, firmly in answer to every excuse or negative answer that comes up. The secret to success here is the calm repetition — most people (not all) give up when they hear the first no. Survey your relationships and you can very quickly discern the number of no statements each one uses to establish or manipulate their way. If someone has five no statements, you repeat your bottom line five times.

It is better not to give your adversary any reason why you want what you want. Reasons weaken your power and can be used to induce guilt. Example: I take my car in Friday to be repaired. When I pick it up, the mechanic says it's fine. It isn't fine, and I respond, "It is not fine and I would like it fixed now." He replies, "I can't right now. Can't you see the people in line before you!" My response is, " I brought the car in Friday. You said it was fine. It is not fine, and I would like you to fix it now." He says, "You are just going to have to wait." I repeat, "I would like you to fix my car now." He says, "You are really selfish," (Guilt). Again I repeat, "I would like you to fix my car now." He responds, "Oh, all right. I'll fix your darn car now."

"I" message (adult) statements in the now. By making clear, straight forward messages, you are quickly understood, and there is less likely to be any confusion about your desires. "I prefer to go to the movies rather than to the ball game." When you assertively give information about yourself and your feelings in response to the other person, you allow for more open, honest communication. This creates a more open feeling for honest response. There is less guessing, assuming, and anxiety.

Clouding. When you are dealing with a very aggressive, heavy parent type, this method allows you to cloud the issue without denying anything or becoming defensive to the attacker. You paraphrase and give him no new information that can be used as the basis for a fight. You (adult) respond simply and calmly, "You could be right about that," acknowledging there could be some truth to what is being said, but you remain in control of what you are going to do. It is like a game of cat and mouse. In reality, you are letting everyone be right for their space, and you are not resorting to aggressive behavior in response, and you are keeping your self-integrity.

Clouding works best when you are not close to the people personally. It sets up a psychological distance for you. This method helps you deal more effectively with criticism in general, as you are less anxious, and it provides your adversary with no rewards at all. For example, your office associate tells you, "You seem to be half asleep on your feet today and your work is not up to par." A clouding response is, "I probably do appear tired, and I guess I could do better work." In this method, you have to listen closely to what your adversary says, but other than that, there is no mental stress involved.

Negative declaration. This method is used when you admit to a mistake without apologizing for it — when you allow someone to be right without arguing. You simply agree with the criticism. The result is you won't have to go through the denial when you reduce their anger or hostility. This helps you go beyond the idea that because you made a mistake, you have to feel guilt or shame. For example: "You were supposed to be here at nine o'clock, and you're always late!" Your response, "You could be right. I seem to be late a lot." Your attacker is attempting to make you feel guilt and anxiety and wants you to crawl because you made a mistake. You are expected to deny any wrongdoing so he can point out every hideous detail of his inconvenience.

Keep in mind there never needs to be any guilt associated with making mistakes, and it is right to not let anyone manipulate your mind into believing otherwise!

Using a negative question in response to a negative assumption. This is used to stop manipulation by attempting to obtain more criticism, so you can use the additional information *if it is of value* to ensure the person gets everything off his chest, and thus, stops all the manipulation ploys. Again, staying in your adult, you question calmly and without emotion. This technique is used more for the people you care about and with whom you want to keep more honest communications. It teaches your critic to be more assertive and less coercive. For example: A husband says to his wife, " I wish you wouldn't go shopping with the girls so often." The wife replies, "What is it that you don't like about me going shopping and having lunch with the girls?" He answers, "Well, the kids miss you a lot at lunch. They would rather have you fix lunch than me!" The wife, "You're right, the kids may miss my nice lunches, but is there anything else that you don't like about it?" The husband answers, "How do I know you are out with the girls. You are very attractive, you know, and some guy might pick you up."

The negative questions can continue until all of the information you need to make an "I" statement is revealed. The wife responds, "I think that the bottom line here is trust, and I assure you I was with the girls, and I can be trusted to be true to you."

Compromise. Another way to handle people who are close to you and trying to manipulate you is to come up with a compromise. This decision, however, must not take away from your self-integrity or you cannot do it. Anything that would cause you to ever consider giving up self-integrity is not acceptable. In a similar scenario, the wife says, "You were wondering if the girls and I really do go to the movies and aren't out partying." Her husband replies, "Yes." As a compromise, the wife suggests, "Why don't you pick us up after the movie and take us to dinner?"

Change the subject. This is one of the methods used on talk shows for an individual to remain in control of the subject. It is done very smoothly. You give a noncommittal or partial answer to the question, and move onto another subject. For example: Host says, "I hear there was a terrible accident in the production of this movie. Can you tell me more?" Guest answers, "Yes, there was a tragic accident, and we all just had to keep going, The movie is very timely and brings people a greater insight on the power of love."

In a family situation — Wife: "I am not feeling well today. Would you stay home and help me? Husband — "If you are not feeling well by tomorrow, I'll call your mother to come over. Did you know I am presenting a project today, and if he buys it, we'll be very well off?"

The secret to using the change of subject technique is to come up with something more interesting than the original topic, something that will stir thoughts and draw attention to another topic. All you are really doing in assertiveness is staying detached and listening to your inner response before you speak in your spiritual adult. This keeps you empowered and in control of your situation. It is all about monitoring the flow of energy.

When you are being assertive, you are coming from the highest, most honest message you can for the situation. That means you express what you see and hear from your own space. Since there is no seeking approval, you are not responsible for another person's reaction.

How to Handle Adverse Reactions to Assertiveness

Certain people do react in a disagreeable manner when they are faced with assertion. If this occurs, stand firm, stay centered (the adult). Backbiting remarks such as "Who do you think you are?" (the child), are best ignored. When you are faced with aggression or temper tantrums, remain consistent and firm. There are times when there might be a psychosomatic reaction. If you are confronting a long-established habit, an actual illness may occur like abdominal pain, headaches, and fainting in the other person. Again, remain firm and consistent in the situation and the other person will soon adjust. Over apologizing or being overly humble is another way people handle confrontation. Simply reassure them that this is totally unnecessary.

Revenge can happen, especially in a continuing relationship — taunting and teasing to make your life miserable. When this takes place, it is important to squelch these reactions immediately. Take the person aside and confront him or her directly.

Chapter Fourteen

Road Map for Relationships

Intimacy is probably the most challenging, and the most reward-ing, aspect of a relationship. To keep the vitality, growth, and unfoldment alive in a long-term partnership, it takes two people to remain unique individuals, and still nurture and support each other on their journey. This is most gratifying. It is harmonizing instead of bondage or blending. It is uplifting and inspiring, instead of negative and destructive. It is giving up judgements, criticisms, opinions, and attitudes, and using assertiveness instead. It is bringing in the Divine Healing energy to guide you and to neutralize misunderstanding and hurts. It is giving up labels in your thinking by more accurately realizing everything as energy — that everything is the law of attraction at work.

Your partner is a reflection of your subconscious. If you are in the male energy mode (mental) in your outer conscious life, your partner is the reflection of your female energy (emotions and feel-ings) in your subconscious. "What around you is you." Your mir-ror is reflecting back your hidden patterns.

To determine where you are in the relationship, an inventory of your six levels (Figure 19) in the now can be very helpful. Remember, you keep changing day by day, so the inventory may change again in six months. Each partner quietly writes as honestly as possible, without seeking approval or trying to read the other person's mind, and comes up with a general idea of what each can contribute to the relationship and what each won't do for the relationship. When each one has completed this

– Figure 19 –

ROAD MAP FOR A RELATIONSHIP
ZONES OR SPACES

NOW	NOW
Spiritual Level	Spiritual Level
Mental Level	Mental Level
Emotional Level	Emotional Level
Physical Level	Physical Level
Social Level	Social Level
Financial Level	Financial Level

Where do you agree? Disagree?

Together Zones • Private Zones • Emotional Zones • Mental Zones
Spiritual Zones • Physical Zones • Social Zones • Financial Zones

Be as honest as you can about your own feelings and thoughts.
Do not get into the other person's space! Maintain your integrity.
Do not seek approval. Talk about differences and how you are going to
handle them. There may be some things that are not open for discussion.
There may be some dynamite (explosive) zones. Be flexible when you can.

What is the goal of this relationship?

Is it worth it?

inventory, it is then time to set up a meeting to discuss these ideas and come up with a road map, of sorts, for living together.

- On the *spiritual level*, each of you is discussing your philosophies, your value system, and then comparing them. Are we compatible on this? If there are major differences, for example religion, you might discuss how to handle them.

- On the *mental level*, do you have common goals? What are the mission statements for your relationship? What decisions are important to you? What areas reflect your integrity, and where is there no compromise? Who is going to be responsible for certain situations such as, who is to decide on the home front? the business? cars? gardening? vacations? entertainment? who does the cooking and grocery shopping? are you going to have children? how many? disciplining the children?

- On the *emotional level*, how reactive are you? What areas are you very sensitive about? How much privacy or space do you require to stay healthy? How much solitude or quiet do you desire? Define your emotional spaces in your home. Do you prefer being left alone between 5 and 7 p.m.? Are you more negative in the morning and need to be left alone? Spell it out! Does constant television wear you out? Agree on how you use the television — sports or soap operas, loud or soft? If these issues are not discussed, they are prime areas for developing hidden resentments.

- On the *physical level*, what kind of life style or home do you want? a condominium? How much room do you need so you are not crammed in? How do you share the bathroom? the closet? the garage? Who takes care of the garden, the yard in general? Remodeling — who decides on changes to be made, colors, fabrics, etc.? Who is responsible for your automotive needs? How tidy are you? Who is going to do the housework? Consider allotted time for shared space.

- On the *social* level, how active or passive a social life do you require? Do you love or hate parties? How many clubs or organizations do you belong to, and how much time is required of you? Sports, exercising? What can be given up

204 / *The Real You* • Irene Hunter

for a while to give quality time to the relationship? How much travelling in business or pleasure? How long is a healthy vacation — a weekend, two weeks, or a month? If you are having overnight guests, what guidelines do you set up so your routines are not totally disrupted? This is an area that most people ignore, and it can create havoc in a home. Whereas, if you were honest enough to tell the guests what works and what doesn't work in your household, they will be happier and so will you because you can go on with your necessary routines. How much time do you spend with extended family? Set quality time boundaries in any relationship.

- On the *financial* level, the key to discussing finances is to remain in your adult and be assertive. In the past, men have generally handled the finances without questions, and women have kept the house and taken care of the children. This is a new world, and each person is to be as self-reliant and self-actualized as possible. Both must participate in the finances and decisions must be made together. Keep current in all aspects of the financial relationships. Credit cards, mortgages, loans, bank accounts, prenuptial agreements, insurance annuities, health care programs, college, lifestyle, income tax, etc. Develop a plan and check on this plan often. This is not the level to go in denial. The consequences are too serious. Also, develop a positive prosperity program to release fear and lack and keep your mind on the answers. Remember, Spirit is the Source of your prosperity consciousness. Don't spend what you don't have!

Other points to consider in your six level inventory are your natural energy rhythms. When are you extroverted or introverted? On a 24-hour cycle, weekly, monthly?

Doing this exercise does so much to bring Light to the relationship. Nothing is left to assumption or mind reading (dangerous at any time!).

Power Trips

Power trips are effective thoughts and emotions from the ego and your reactions to the energies around you. Acting manipulative and dictatorial, you use power trips to set up plans for someone else's behavior. It is a control issue that takes away another's choice and freedom. It is making decisions from assumptions — dangerous at any time. Power trips are also avoidance and denial, blaming others for your feelings instead of taking responsibility for your own actions. You create guilt and blame in the other person.

The following three categories sum up power trips.

1. *Agenda.* (Figure 20) What plans do you make for the other person? This can often create resentment and hostility.

2. *Expectations.* Here is where mythical thinking takes place and truly sets you up for disappointment. Don't take anything for granted. For example, "I just know he is going to ask me to dinner tonight. I'll buy a new dress!" It didn't happen. He didn't call, and she blew her budget on a false expectation. Get her into your adult "I" message, and check out the plan.

3. *Projections* are often more subtle, like putting blame on the other person for your own anger. Maybe you project your guilt on the partner, knowing your partner will punish you, and you can feel vindicated. When you feel negative energy in your aura or are uncomfortable and you know you are not centered, check it out to see what's happening. Ask yourself where this anger is coming from. Is it a projection expressed toward you from someone else? This is why it is so important to stay detached so you can monitor the flow of energy.

Priorities

Priorities set up healthy boundaries that support you on your life journey and develop your individuality. Priorities follow the natural order of life creating function and flow. All decisions are based on the fundamental laws of spiritual growth.

– Figure 20 –

POWER TRIPS
AGENDAS • EXPECTATIONS • PROJECTIONS

Boundary

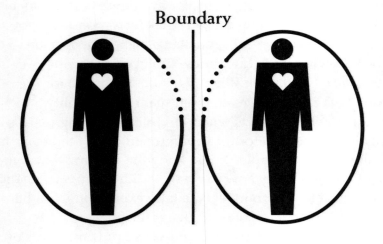

	Priorities:
First, cause:	1. Self
	2. Work or self-expression
Then, effect:	3. Relationships

The first priority is your uniqueness, the Real You. There is only one in the universe, and that is you. There is no other. What you are seeing is a mirror reflection of your consciousness. You know who you are by what is revealed to you through your five senses. This tells you where you are in growth and unfoldment. It is of prime importance to be true to you, then all else falls into place. It is vital that you do this to sustain integrity. Being true to yourself also maintains Divine Balance, Divine Harmony, Divine Order, and Divine Timing in the now. When you make a decision to please someone else, it throws everything out of balance and harmony. It is dishonest. That's why assertive communication skills are so crucial to your well-being — to keep you from being confused or out of synchronicity so you can deliver an honest, clear message. The energies around you then can respond in their truth, and it keeps everyone on the spiritual path. What this really means is that you have great self-esteem and self-acceptance.

The second priority is your self-expression or your work. This sustains self-esteem and self-acceptance. This priority is Spirit expressing through you as you. More creates more, and Spirit is always becoming more of Itself through your demonstrations in life. It is never stagnant or static, It is always expanding. When you obey this work ethic, you have something to bring to a relationship, and yet it sustains independence.

The effect or result of these priorities creates a healthy energy for relationships. Relationships must be number three. If you place relationships in the number one position, you lose yourself, then the power structure weakens and is distorted. If you are not self-actualized, there is nothing to contribute to the well-being of the relationship, and both energies lose. This may sound selfish on the surface, but follow it through, and you will see how great it works for the benefit of everyone.

The most important relationship in your life is the one you have with your spiritual self — The Real You. You are a natural born winner, and you have everything within yourself right now to be and become! It is your life work to reveal the Perfect

Power and Perfect Presence by living by the inner laws of love and by revealing the patterns that you came to express. You are precious energy in the universe, and letting your Light shine, you bring peace, prosperity, wholeness, harmony, and joy to the world, moment to moment.

Bibliography

The Power of Decision, Dr. Raymond Charles Barker
Games People Play, Dr. Eric Berne
Levels, Nancy M. Brannon
Light Emerging, Barbara Ann Brennan
Ageless Body, Timeless Mind, Deepak Chopra, M.D.
An Easy Guide to Meditation, Roy Eugene Davis
Transcendental Meditation, Marharishi Mahesh Yogi and Jack Forem
I'm OK — You're OK, Thomas A. Harris, M.D.
The Science of Mind, Ernest Holmes
This Thing Called You, Ernest Holmes
Feel the Fear and Do It Anyway, Susan Jeffers, Ph.D.
Your Life Is A Gift, Ken Keys, Jr.
The Power of Your Subconscious Mind, Dr. Joseph Murphy
Pray and Grow Rich, Catherine Ponder
When I Say No, I Feel Guilty, Manuel J. Smith, Ph.D.
You, Francis Wilshire

Irene Amanda Hunter
Teacher, Lecturer, Author

Irene Hunter was raised on the prairies and on the mountain slopes of western Canada. She married and moved to a wheat ranch in Montana, where her two sons were born. Here, she became a naturalized United States citizen.

Her career has been multifaceted — secretary, fashion model, and director of education of a career college, and she has attained her private pilot license. Some outdoor activities in which she has participated are sky diving, water skiing, camping, horseback riding, and boating.

For the past three decades, Irene has studied with many of the world's great teachers in self-actualization, motivation, and metaphysics.

In her own unique approach, known as "The Real You," she has synthesized this material to live life dynamically. Thousands of students have found this as the doorway to great changes in their lives.

Other Real You Seminars and Workshops
Taught by Irene Amanda Hunter

■ The Real You Self-Acceptance Seminar

Self acceptance is the very basis of every action that takes place in your day-to-day living. When you care for you, understand your power, your strengths and weaknesses, you make wiser decisions for your growth. How much of your day is spent as a victim of someone else's decisions? Uncontrolled emotional responses can wreck your life. Learn how to turn this powerful energy for positive creative results now!

This is a 10-hour class of developing the basic concepts of individuality, identity, and self-awareness. Techniques in meditation, affirmation, use of imagery, how to ask for a change of behavior, and your bill of rights are given. These lessons are diagrams for creative living, for generating your support system, and for establishing self-reliance.

■ The Power Series — Dynamic!

Now you can utilize the most effective pathway to mastership by a deeper understanding of your power! Become free of all limitations and illusions to live every moment of every day, exemplifying the full expression of your Higher Self. Learn the timeless wisdom of the Masters, which unfolds inner happiness, new freedom, and positive control as never before. This series is to refine the metaphysical principles that you know now. Develop the winning state of mind.

Subjects of this 10-hour Power Series are the power of love and law, the power of the word, the power of decisions, the power of a winner, the power of work, the power of time, the power of prosperity, the power of relationships, five steps of change, and more. It's all about empowerment and change.

■ New Explorations in Communication and Personal Growth

The goal of this workshop is to develop better communication skills to get in touch with your Inner Self, and then apply these skills in your relationship to life — people, places, and things. Once you realize personality patterns, you can take charge of the negative and positive energy and direct it to a single purpose of abundant good.

Techniques used are journaling, inner dialoguing, revealing subpersonalities, child-adult separation, assertive skills, and updating your goals.

This is a successful way to release the burden of the past and allow your good to flow. The greatest benefit from this class is to be able to communicate what you see, feel, and hear honestly without fear and to trust that truth to bring you to your highest good (no more games). It includes tools to evaluate and update your life-style. This 10-hour class is wonderful for couples.

■ The Way of Transformation

By understanding your energy system, you can transform your life. When you focus on your inner order, balance, rhythm, and harmony, you automatically create peace, poise, and prosperity for a greater state of being. The 20-hour study includes cosmic consciousness, aura, chakras, psychic energy and how to handle it, hypnosis, astrology, reincarnation, where to place these energies in decision making, proper use of concentration, the art of self-control, dialoguing with subpersonalities, making peace with your parents, assertiveness tools, chemicalization, how to meditate properly, the use of spiritual mind treatment, dreams, and much more.

■ Dreams, The Magic Mirror

This is a multidimensional adventure in understanding the 24-hour life energy cycle and using sleep time as another doorway to personal creativity and for practical ways to problem solve. Techniques for this 6-hour course are how to understand personal dream symbols, explanation of out-of-body travel, dream telepathy, past lives revealed in dreams, the Senoian Dream method for resolving conflict, lucid dreaming, and a guided day dream. Dream consulting available.

■ Put Weight in Its Proper Place

This is a chance to reveal the choices — mental, emotional, and physical — that are made to create weight. Dialogue with the body, the fat self, the thin self, the real you, and study your parent, adult, and child. A plan of action to heal this misplaced energy.

The 10-hour workshop includes tools to create a new you, the Real You. Learn wardrobe principles, figure analysis, color principles, body posture, how to walk, sit, and enter a car and a room, mantra meditation, energy field, chakras, and more.

■ The Real You Teens

This course gives teenagers a good foundation for the rest of their lives. They are given skills and tools to problem solve, to discover that for every problem they have an answer. They get an insight into their own unique abilities and are encouraged to develop a deep sense of self-acceptance. A one-day seminar, it includes brief lectures, questions and answers, class participation and exercises to demonstrate the dynamics taught. Brown bag lunch.

Ongoing Workshops

■ Issues and Answers

The Acorn Society, graduates of The Real You Seminars, meet the first Tuesday of the month to discuss issues and answers. This is a chance to clarify your tools, ask questions you always wanted to in class, and plan your strategy for getting where you want to go. Perhaps a book or a dream pursued can be discussed.

This is a lively discussion group. The sessions are closed with a very special technique of spiritual mind treatment, a method of clearing the mind to demonstrate your heart's desires.

Class is from 7 p.m. to 9 p.m. Please call for a reservation.

Private Conferences

■ Irene Hunter also provides private conferences to:

- Assist you in your journey for your personal growth
- Develop your use of the tools in the techniques and the principles of the teaching.
- Coaching you in communication skills and decision making.
- Power enhancement for managing meetings and dealing with people
- A mentor for monitoring your right state of mind to be the winner you were born to be!

■ Conferences can be held in person or by telephone

1 hour conference (50 minutes)
½ hour conference (25 minutes)

■ Private conferences can be schedule with Irene by:

Telephone: 602.840.3331
Email: therealyou@irenehunter.com or
             irenehunter@cox.net
Fax: 602.795.8596

The Real You Cassettes

■ **The Miracle of Being The Real You:**
Mind Dynamics for Personality Evolvement
This is a taped version of the book *The Miracle of Being The Real You*.

Album: 6 cassette tapes, approximately 7½ hours.

$35 plus Arizona sales tax

The Real You is professionally taped and edited, contains 7½ hours of of this life-changing course. It includes techniques and principles to use as guidelines through life's journeys.

This is a convenience for the serious student, either to prepare in advance of classes or to refer to after classes as reassurance of the proper use of skills.

With or without the seminar, these tapes are a terrific tool to assist in a personal journey.

Order Form

Yes, please send me the following items:

☐ **THE MIRACLE OF BEING THE REAL YOU BOOK** $17.95 x _____ = _____

☐ **THE MIRACLE OF BEING THE REAL YOU**
  CASSETTE ALBUM $35.00 x _____ = _____

Subtotal = $_____

Arizona residents add 8.1% tax = $_____

Please add $3.99 shipping/handling for the first book or cassette,
plus $1.50 for each additional item.
Canadian orders: $4.25 for shipping/handling,
plus $2.95 for each additional item.

Shipping = $_____

Total = $_____

Payment must accompany all orders — U.S. dollars only

Ship to:

Name_____

Street_____

City _____

State_____

Zip _____

Area Code (   ) Telephone _____

Make checks or money orders payable to:
Irene Hunter

Mail to:
5612 North Camelback Canyon Drive
Phoenix, Arizona 85018

Further Information

For additonal information, write Irene Hunter at:

The Real You Seminars
5612 North Camelback Canyon Drive
Phoenix, Arizona 85018

Telephone:
(602) 840-3331
(Please leave your name, address with zip code,
and telephone number on the answering tape.)

Email: irenehunter@cox.net
Fax: (602) 795-8596
website: www.irenehunter.com